THE NATIONAL CURRICULUM OUTDOORS

YEAR 3

A complete scheme of work

**Deborah Lambert,
Michelle Roberts and Sue Waite**

BLOOMSBURY

BLOOMSBURY EDUCATION

Bloomsbury Publishing Plc

50 Bedford Square, London, WC1B 3DP, UK

BLOOMSBURY, BLOOMSBURY EDUCATION and the Diana logo are trademarks of
Bloomsbury Publishing Plc

First published in Great Britain, 2020 by Bloomsbury Publishing Plc

A catalogue record for this book is available from the British Library

ISBN: PB: 978-1-4729-6662-9; ePDF 978-1-4729-8436-4; Shutterstock

2 4 6 8 10 9 7 5 3 1

Printed and bound in the UK by Ashford Colour Press

Dedication

We dedicate this book to all teachers who are willing to take their teaching outside the classroom
and offer exciting learning opportunities, foster positive health and wellbeing outcomes and
connect children with their natural environment. They are our hope for an education for excellence
and sustainability.

We also dedicate it to Deborah's mum Jennifer Lilley for her support and guidance, her brother
Jason Lilley for his shared passion for Art and her partner, Andy Rimmer for his patience and
support throughout the writing process, to Michelle's partner Andy Mitchell for his continued
support and excellent photographs and to her nephew and niece Robbie and Alice, who have
inspired many of the KS2 ideas alongside Coads Green Primary School and to Sue's family,
fellow committed nature and learning lovers.

Contents

Photos and further resources

Illustrative photos and further resources are
available online at
www.bloomsbury.com/NC-Outdoors.

Acknowledgements

This book has been inspired by the children who have shown us their wonder and excitement at discovering and learning in the outdoors. We would like to acknowledge the many writers and organisations that have shared ideas to promote experiential activities for children, and the policymakers that are making changes that support this movement.

Michelle and Deborah were encouraged to write this book having worked for the last five years on the development and delivery of the Wild Tribe outdoor learning programme. This is an outdoor learning programme developed in South East Cornwall and is now part of The West Country Schools Trust, with the intention of engaging teachers and children in learning through the outdoors. Through this programme, more than 250 teachers have now been trained in outdoor learning, with many thousands of children now receiving outdoor learning on a weekly basis. This programme is being extended nationally in partnership with other schools across the country. Wild Tribe was a pivotal partner in the Natural Connections Demonstration project, and we are grateful to Natural England, the Department for the Environment, Food and Rural Affairs, and Historic England for funding that project. Sue led Natural Connections, working with over 125 schools across the South West to embed curricular learning in local natural environments. Learning from the project has influenced the development of the 'nature friendly schools' initiative, part of DEFRA's 25-year plan (DEFRA, 2018).

We are especially indebted to Helen Blackburn based at West Country Schools Trust for the brilliant set of progressions for Year 3 History. Also to Kayleigh Halifax from the West Country Schools Trust for providing some inspirational ideas for the KS2 music chapter.

Foreword

As adults, when we reflect upon our education and the value of what we learned during our years at school, a variety of memories and associated emotions surface. We tend to recall with more clarity the outdoor experiences we had compared with our time inside. This may have been school trips, residentials or what our playtimes were like. The practical subjects, such as woodwork, home economics and art, and what you learned in these classes have probably stuck in your mind more than which aspect of maths you were working on in January of Year 5.

Thus, integrating practical, creative and outdoor experiences into our ordinary, everyday school lives is a route to profoundly changing children's memories and perceptions of the learning that happens. The evidence is growing year on year for the benefits of learning and playing outside, particularly when this happens in a natural space. It is no longer simply a 'jolly good thing' to do. There is a fundamental shift happening in education as we recognise that our mainstream schools need to be more responsive to children and the complex world in which they live. This is part of a wider understanding of how children learn and what they need in their lives to help them gain the emotional resilience and flexibility to adapt and cope with what life will throw at them.

One of the key challenges facing primary teachers is knowing what to teach outside and how. These books positively address both matters. The authors take a systematic approach that enables teachers to plan and deliver a series of lessons in many different subject areas. The lessons are designed to be undertaken in a range of different contexts, so you are not relying on a beautiful beach or perfect school grounds or to find a willing volunteer to dress up as a Roman soldier to ensure success.

The authors have incorporated the use of tools and techniques that deepen the learning beyond the core skills, knowledge and understanding within the National Curriculum. As part of the array of lessons presented, children are learning how to be outside, to take in what is happening and to develop a sensitivity and positive regard for the natural and built world in which we live.

This book is a timely and welcome addition to help primary teachers grow their confidence and competence to undertake great teaching – outdoors!

Juliet Robertson

Creative STAR learning (www.creativestarlearning.co.uk)

Why teach outdoors in Year 3?

Research has shown that from the Early Years Foundation Stage to Key Stage 1 (KS1) there is a marked decline in opportunities for children to learn outside the classroom (Waite, 2010). These opportunities are even further reduced when children enter Key Stage 2 (KS2) and yet children still value outdoor learning. By continuing outdoor teaching and learning, KS2 teachers can capitalise on earlier learning practice while gradually introducing more challenge. There is a wealth of research that shows how beneficial learning outside the classroom is for making knowledge, understanding and skills stick.

Embedding teaching outdoors into your practice

It is increasingly recognised that creative and challenging outdoor learning activities develop personal, social and thinking skills, communication, problem-solving and teamwork, breadth of understanding and an introduction to the essential knowledge that children need to develop into confident and responsible citizens who value and appreciate the natural environment around them.

But this raises questions such as: Should 'outdoor learning' be treated as a separate subject or can it rather be a valuable teaching method that enables teachers and children to meet National Curriculum requirements across different disciplines? Is it possible to integrate curriculum learning with an outdoor learning pedagogic approach that enables teachers and children to meet National Curriculum requirements through the medium of the outdoors? Structured outdoor activities linked to the curriculum provide a depth and relevance that can be difficult to achieve indoors. Ofsted recognises that well-informed teachers can plan outdoor learning programmes that enable pupils to take part in a range of exciting curriculum-linked activities that not only develop self-confidence and self-esteem, but also enable them to manage risk and contribute to developing spiritual, moral, social and cultural understanding. (See, for example, the 2018 Ofsted report for Holsworthy Primary School in Devon.)

Benefits

There has been a long history of children learning through playful engagement with the environment outside the classroom in the Foundation Stage (age three to five years), following in the footsteps of early childhood education pioneers such as Susan Isaacs, Margaret McMillan and Friedrich Froebel (Garrick, 2004). Evidence also points to hands-on experiential learning in natural environments contributing to other key learning factors (Waite et al., 2016), promoting improved creativity, engagement and understanding (Rowe and Humphries, 2012).

The need to continue promoting these fundamental learning building blocks does not suddenly cease at age five, or indeed at seven years of age; they underpin successful learning at any age. A 2019 study showed that children and young people, particularly those from lower socioeconomic backgrounds, would prefer to have more practical hands-on subject teaching in their schooling (Araneda, Guzmán and Nussbaum, 2019).

The pedagogies that encourage these building blocks require chances to grapple with questions that don't necessarily have one correct answer, better reflecting the complexity of the world that faces us all outside the classroom. Asking not just 'what' but 'how' and 'why' and 'what might be done about it' encourages critical thinking and problem-solving skills; while teamwork and collaboration acknowledge that others may think differently and that we need to be able to take diverse views and strengths into account.

The value of outdoor learning on children's health and wellbeing, as well as in stimulating their natural curiosity about the world, has been recognised by researchers (Wood et al., 2016; Morgan and Waite, 2017) and policy-makers here and abroad (DEFRA, 2018; Ho, 2014). As the Institute for Outdoor Learning (2018) states:

> *At a time when we are increasingly concerned about the physical and emotional wellbeing of our children and young people, and question whether they will leave education with the skills and competencies they will need for the future, outdoor learning brings with it a range of benefits which are now widely evidenced, acknowledged and accepted.*

The Natural Connections Demonstration project, a large-scale study across 125 schools in the South West of England, found that staff in over 70 per cent of participating schools reported heightened health and wellbeing for themselves, with 80 per cent reporting that their practice was enhanced by delivering more teaching outdoors (Waite et al., 2016). Education outdoors is healthy practice – not just for the pupils!

Moreover, Public Health England has recommended green exercise and nature experiences as preventive strategies to counteract many contemporary physical and mental health challenges that children and young people face (PHE, 2014a; DHSC, 2018), with the school context being identified as a universal access point to deliver these key learning benefits to those who might otherwise miss out (Natural England, 2013). There is an evidenced link between whole-school approaches that transform schools' ethos and environment for outdoor learning and improvements in pupils' social and emotional skills and their physical health (PHE, 2014b). These benefits can be achieved via a recognised pathway to impact on pupil attainment through increasing the regularity and quality of outdoor learning (Waite et al., 2016).

Figure 1: The pathway to raised attainment through outdoor learning (Waite et al., 2016, p. 10)

Figure 1 illustrates that by enabling children to engage with different learning contexts and methods, teaching outdoors can bring improvement in attainment and other key desirable outcomes, broadly identified as falling into the following categories:

- healthy bodies and lifestyles

- social, confident and connected people

- self-directed learning skills

- effective contributors and collaborators

- concerned active citizens.

(Malone and Waite, 2016)

Yet despite this wealth of positive evidence, there is a substantial waning of opportunities to benefit from learning outdoors as children move through primary school.

Challenges

Perhaps the greatest perceived barrier to teaching outdoors is the weather. However, the prevalence and success of outdoor play and learning in colder and wetter climes, such as Scandinavia, suggests that the real challenge is to be properly dressed. Getting parents informed and on board and providing waterproof kit and wellies can help to overcome this. Teachers also need to be well prepared, so that they are comfortable whatever the weather. Surprisingly, weather was not found to be a major barrier in the Natural Connections Demonstration project. The main challenges (and solutions) to outdoor learning that the project identified fell into three main themes:

- **People-related**, with issues often centred around staff confidence to teach outdoors; these were overcome by the use of whole-school approaches, supported by positive leadership and by demonstrating and sharing clearly what had been done, why (the intent) and what had been learned.

- **Place-related**, with the provision of easily accessible and suitable outdoor learning areas within a setting; for example, including ground works in school improvement plans played a key part in embedding outdoor curricular learning.

- **Policy-related**, with schools reporting difficulties in balancing outdoor learning with other dominant performance measures, such as a dependence on written records for assessment, especially if outdoor learning was perceived as an additional activity rather than an enriching one (see also the chapter 'Assessment outdoors').

Over the course of the Natural Connections Demonstration project, the majority of teachers overcame a variety of barriers to taking learning outdoors, as they strongly appreciated its value for children's:

- enjoyment of lessons

- engagement with and understanding of nature

- social skills

- engagement with learning

- health and wellbeing

- behaviour

- attainment.

Teachers wanted support in linking outdoor activities to the National Curriculum in order to maximise the time available to teach outdoors (Edwards-Jones, Waite & Passy, 2017). Our response to this has been the creation of *The National Curriculum Outdoors* series of books, showcasing how outdoor learning can be delivered as an integral part of the school curriculum delivery with the provision of a clear set of lesson plans explaining not only the 'what' but 'how' they can be delivered. This provides children with the opportunity to experience outdoor learning, while their teachers grow in knowledge and confidence.

As outdoor learning becomes established throughout your primary school, it is worth remembering that not all outdoor learning needs to happen in the school grounds. Identifying other local green spaces can extend the possibilities for learning, provide opportunities for progression in experience of different natural environments and help to make use by all classes of outdoor learning areas more sustainable. A mix of familiar and new places offer complementary support for health and wellbeing and environmental awareness.

How to use this book

This book offers support to KS2 practitioners in terms of how to take the National Curriculum outdoors, by providing well-structured, motivating, relevant and accessible progressions especially planned for children as they move through KS2, using local outdoor spaces to enhance teaching and learning and help make it memorable. The progressions include detailed teacher-directed activities to build confidence in teaching outdoors, linking this to National Curriculum content. The content throughout the progressions gradually builds on knowledge, concepts and understanding to enable all pupils to make progress from their individual starting points; activities are repeated in different contexts to provide opportunities for pupils to practise what they know in order to deepen their understanding. However, the intention is to use pedagogical approaches that will offer chances for children to initiate and follow their own lines of enquiry. These 'squirrel moments', when something unanticipated happens in the natural environment and captures the children's imagination, form a valuable element in teaching and learning outside and are well worth capitalising upon (Waite et al., 2006).

The progressions provide six structured sessions for each of the core subjects of English, mathematics and science and the foundation subjects of art and design, design and technology, geography and history, along with religious education and a language (French). Music is covered in a whole KS2 set of progressions.

Set in the autumn term, to provide a consistent point in the academic year from which to reinforce and build on previous learning experiences, the progressions enable schools and teachers to deliver activities that have been carefully planned to support progression across a single year group in Key Stage 2, aligning with the content of prescribed programmes of study and attainment targets of the 2014 National Curriculum. The context for the outdoor learning is also generally assumed to be the school grounds or natural environments within easy walking distance to maximise learning time. However, as we advised earlier, progression in terms of the places in which children learn should also be considered. At KS2, it would be valuable to include more varied and distant locations for field trips and residential visits, contributing to children's development and understanding of their place in the world (Waite, 2013; York Consulting, 2015).

Questions posed throughout the progressions provide continuous 'assessment for learning' opportunities, promoting a deeper level of understanding in line with Ofsted expectations.

Is anything missing?

Progressions for physical education and computing are not included in this book. However, all progressions offer opportunities for increased physical activity and lowered levels of sedentary behaviour (Aronsson et al., 2015) and for satisfying physical education objectives in part. There are also many opportunities to apply computing objectives back in the classroom, following outdoor sessions, using 'technology purposefully to create, organise, store, manipulate and retrieve digital content' (DfE, 2014) within many of the subjects (Opie, Ansell & Goto, 2017).

Personal, social, health and economic education (PSHE) is a non-statutory subject on the school curriculum. However, Section 2.5 of the National Curriculum (DfE, 2014) states that all state schools 'should make provision for personal, social, health and economic

education, drawing on good practice', and this has been strengthened in line with recommendations about mental health and wellbeing (National Health Service (England), 2018), with trailblazer schools in the Link Programme testing methods during 2019. Activities within the progressions that encourage effective social interaction and independent, creative and critical thinking provide coverage of key PSHE objectives, with many of these opportunities highlighted under the 'health and wellbeing' section in the introduction of each unit.

The 'natural connections' sections, also in the introduction to each unit, show how children's attention can be focused on the natural world, increasing awareness, care and understanding to develop feelings of being a 'part of nature' and engendering responsibility for environmental stewardship, alongside the curricular-based learning. Further opportunities to follow up children's interests in, or draw attention to, their environment will naturally emerge when teaching outside the classroom. Together with changes in pedagogical approach, the overarching themes of health and wellbeing and natural connections will help to form a thread of education for sustainability throughout the curriculum (Green and Somerville, 2015; Bourn et al., 2016).

Conclusion

The expectation is that teachers will still wish to adapt these plans to their own contexts, but much of the time-consuming work of thinking through rationales, curricular links, health and safety, assessment and resources has been taken care of, so that more time is available to extend and develop personal or school-wide ideas and practice. One important aspect to bear in mind is the centrality of stimulating curious minds and offering choice and autonomy when teaching outside the classroom so that children accept responsibility for and want to drive their learning. Developing self-regulated learning habits and intrinsic motivation will provide strong foundations for success at secondary and higher education stages.

There are many superb additional resources online linked to curriculum subjects from organisations such as the Wildlife Trusts, Woodland Trust, Council for Learning Outside the Classroom and Field Studies Council. With careful planning and experience, these and ideas in books such as Juliet Robertson's *Dirty Teaching*, Jo Schofield and Fiona Danks' *The Stick Book* and Marina Robb, Victoria Mew and Anna Richardson's *Learning with Nature* are great sources of other activity ideas that, with experience, can be linked effectively to the curriculum. *Educating Outside* by Helen Porter also has some great curriculum-linked ideas to expand your repertoire over time.

Our aim with this book has been to provide progressions over six sessions with clearly identified curriculum content. We hope that using this book and its companions for Key Stage 2 will be only the start of some really exciting teaching outdoors for you, your pupils and your school.

Assessment outdoors

Part of our impetus for writing this book was the acknowledgement that, with changes to curriculum policy and the emphasis being placed on recording learning, schools need to provide evidence that they know *why* key curriculum content is included, *whether* the curriculum is being implemented effectively and *what* impact their outdoor curriculum is having on pupils' knowledge and understanding. A 2018 report that informed the greater concentration in the new Ofsted inspection framework on curriculum intent, implementation and impact noted:

> ... the main focus was on putting a plan together, but not checking the implementation of that plan effectively enough. This was linked to an onus on delivering the content of the national curriculum for foundation subjects, but without careful thought given to the progression of knowledge and skill that would make this useful learning for pupils. (Ofsted, 2018, p. 15)

Ofsted inspectors reported that the most telling indicators of curriculum quality were a coherent rationale, knowledge of curriculum concepts and an ambitious curriculum. Subject leadership knowledge, a progression model and robust assessment of the curriculum were also vital (Ofsted, 2018). As far as we know, this is the first book to support teachers in meeting all these criteria when teaching the curriculum outside.

Assessment has two main functions: first as a guide to planning the next steps for the children, i.e. assessment *for* learning, and second to summarise what a pupil has learned, i.e. assessment *of* learning. The latter, summative assessment, such as end-of-unit or key stage tests, provides evidence of levels of understanding and secure knowledge of content. As Waite et al. (2015) note, there are two aspects to robust tracking of a child's learning journey:

1. children's achievement of lesson objectives

2. an evaluation of the impact of lesson activities.

This enables teaching and learning to build productively on what has gone before, with awareness of what has worked well and which concepts or skills may need other approaches. We address both these aspects in the carefully structured progressions in this book, providing clear learning objectives linked to the National Curriculum content, together with evaluation prompts

through open questioning about the activities. Linking to the National Curriculum content provides each session with subject-specific criteria against which the success of taking the learning outside may be measured, reassuring Ofsted and school leadership that teaching outdoors offers valuable curricular learning opportunities.

Throughout each progression, pupils are encouraged to consider and explain their own successes or failures to themselves and to take responsibility for their own learning (Hawe and Parr, 2014). They are guided towards the recognition that some factors that lead to success or failure are controllable, such as the tools and materials suiting the task, how much they are interested in the task or how much effort they put into making it a success. Other factors may not be so controllable, such as the weather or the need for adult support and supervision. Children are encouraged to learn to attribute successes and failures to controllable factors, and to develop a clear idea of what good work looks like and what they need to do to reach this standard (Weiner, 1986; Dweck, 2008). These curricular learning opportunities are underpinned by a range of pedagogical strategies (Paniagua and Istance, 2018), such as experiential learning, encouraging pupil autonomy, independent and group working, and self-regulation of learning (Educational Endowment Foundation, 2018).

The adult role

The adults supporting learning are encouraged to model the activity themselves, acknowledging the tricky parts, recognising difficulty and being positive about the management of any difficulties. If the adult presents mistakes as an opportunity for learning, the children will start to see that it is possible to learn from failure, to keep trying, to try different or creative approaches or to tackle the problem from a different perspective. This develops children's resilience and perseverance in the face of problems. Allowing such experimentation and creativity, coupled with teachers' use and repetition of questions, encourages the use of new vocabulary to clarify meaning in context, and adds depth and breadth to children's learning experiences. The adult has overall responsibility for safety, but it is equally important that they know when to step back and encourage children to think for themselves, solve problems and be creative. Outdoor spaces have been shown to facilitate more autonomy in and self-regulation of learning (Bølling et al., 2018).

Across the units, activities are repeated in different contexts, providing reinforcement and deepening or layering of knowledge so the children can build upon previous knowledge and experiences, and offering the chance to gauge improvement over time. The sections on prior learning in the session plans aid progression and provide opportunities for mastery. Teachers can thus make judgements about whether pupils are 'exploring', 'meeting' or 'exceeding', 'emerging – expected – exceeding' or 'working towards', 'working at' or 'working beyond' targeted levels of knowledge and understanding.

Supporting special educational needs and disability

An important part of assessment is to enable school staff to tailor teaching and support effectively so that all pupils can access and achieve across the curriculum. Every unit in this book includes advice on how to adapt practices to make them more inclusive and extend learning. The space, task, equipment and people (STEP) approach can be adopted throughout the book. By changing the space, task, equipment or people, the activity can be made more challenging or easier to understand, enabling all pupils to take part. For example:

1. Consider the **space** the children will be working in: is it well-resourced and accessible, with distractions minimised?

2. Does the **task** need to be simplified or scaffolded or need adult support, or should it be extended to stretch the most able and talented children?

3. Consider the **resources**: are they accessible and suitable for the purpose, or do they need to be simplified or made more challenging in some way? Does equipment need to be smaller, lighter or adapted in some way?

4. Think about the **people** that could support better adaptations. Consult the pupil about the kind and level of support they need, e.g. by buddying up or working independently. Seek advice from the special educational needs and/or disability coordinator if in doubt. Consider how adult roles might be shaped to facilitate experiences of autonomy and challenge.

The STEP approach was developed by the Training and Development Agency for Schools (TDA, 2009, Appendix A, pp. 29–31).

Gathering the evidence

Maynard et al. (2013, p. 295) found that some teachers struggled 'with documenting children's learning particularly given the perceived need to meet statutory curriculum requirements'. However, many techniques used by colleagues in Early Years in outdoor contexts can be used at later stages of children's education.

Examples can include taking photos of the learning process, including children measuring, collecting specimens or creating pictograms using natural materials. Selecting and annotating photos back in the classroom provides the opportunity for written records or to apply computing objectives, using 'technology purposefully to create, organise, store, manipulate and retrieve digital content' (DfE, 2014). It can also serve as a visual summative record, evidencing which parts of the curriculum have been experienced and mastered.

Opportunities to address children's connection to the natural environment and health and wellbeing outcomes have been included under 'Natural connections' and 'Health and wellbeing' in the introductions to each set of progressions in this book. Other methods that can help to assess improvements in pupils' health and wellbeing include, for example, resources in Wright et al.'s (2016) *Creating Happy and Healthy Schools through Outdoor Learning*. Teachers and children can report physical activity and happiness levels using simple questionnaires developed through research, enabling schools to monitor the contributions of lessons to pupils' health and wellbeing. Assessment of children's connection to nature can also be used to explore the effects of increasing outdoor teaching and learning on children's environmental values; see, for example, Hunt et al.'s (2017, p. 60) 'Nature Connectedness Scale'.

End-of-unit or key stage summative assessment tests can provide evidence of children's levels of understanding and secure subject knowledge. However, assessing learning through the provision of carefully planned activities, through the use of open questioning for self-assessment and by providing positive and constructive task-focused adult and peer feedback can help shape student understanding across their learning, thus encouraging children to become more involved in their learning processes and gain in confidence as they acquire a deeper awareness of where they are and where they want to be in their learning and achievement. It can also provide clearer insight into the skills and processes that children are using in their learning within subject disciplines, which will form the basis of later development and progress in that subject.

Integrated and progressive assessment

Evidence of learning can thus be gathered wherever it occurs, together with an appreciation of all that can be achieved in outdoor contexts. In many units, we have included classroom extensions such as compiling interactive displays, which will demonstrate learning over the course of progressions. Joining up learning inside and outside the classroom also helps to ensure that assessment happens in a variety of contexts, reinforcing and consolidating knowledge, skills and understanding. Assessment reflecting pupil achievement resulting from teaching and learning outdoors will help schools to recognise that learning can and does take place anywhere – that outdoor learning is not an 'extra' but can be integral to the delivery of the National Curriculum and can contribute to school priorities, including attainment and progression (Waite, Passy and Gilchrist, 2014).

Health and safety outdoors

Children are spending more and more time inside, with a 2018 survey of 2,000 parents reporting that children aged six to 16 only spent about seven hours outside each week in total, but more than twice that time just playing video games indoors (OnePoll, 2018). One of the reasons for writing this book was to inspire and encourage teachers and teaching assistants to take learning outdoors, thus offering and promoting children's experiences of natural environments. Teaching curriculum subjects outdoors not only offers children a range of different ways of learning but also enables them to experience success in different contexts, offering the opportunity to raise the confidence and aspirations of all children, but particularly those who may struggle inside the classroom.

One of the biggest perceived barriers to teaching outdoors is often identified as concerns over health and safety. In this chapter, we provide advice and guidance about safe practice for lead practitioners, aiming to promote the safe delivery of outdoor learning in order to meet current health and safety guidance. In a primary school setting, it is ultimately the responsibility of the headteacher to ensure that activities delivered on the school site are safe and follow best practice, but everyone, including the children, should take some responsibility for assessing risks and managing them appropriately.

The law

In simple terms, the law requires those responsible to take reasonable steps to ensure that the risks are at an acceptable level. As stated by the Department for Education, health and safety law requires the school to assess risks and put in place proportionate control measures (DfE, 2018a). The key task is to carry out a 'suitable and sufficient risk assessment' and to act on its findings. What counts as 'suitable and sufficient' – for instance, the type of risk assessment, the level of detail and whether or not it is written down – depends on the circumstances. However, what is expected is a *proportionate* approach. The Health and Safety Executive (HSE, 2018) makes it clear that health and safety is not about generating excessive paperwork (Gill, 2016). The DfE (2018a) also states that schools must have a health and safety policy. Health and safety outdoors should form part of your outdoor learning policy, and also include the implications of teaching outdoors for your behaviour management and safeguarding policies. There are many online resources that support schools in developing an outdoor learning policy. An example template with associated guidance can be found on the Council for Learning Outside the Classroom site (www. lotc.org.uk/plan-deliver-lotc/policy-and-curriculum-planning).

Assessing risks and benefits

A risk assessment is a key prerequisite for planning teaching outdoors that should be included in the outdoor learning policy. It will be something that most teachers are familiar with from planning school trips, and it does not mean that all risks need to be eliminated. The outdoor learning policy should set out the roles and responsibilities within the risk-management processes, the mechanisms to control risk and specific control measures that need to be put in place. However, risk assessments should always balance benefits against potential hazards (Waite, Wickett and Huggins, 2014).

> " *Risk-benefit management is a fundamental part of life and is a skill needed for young people's safety and wellbeing. Staff have a duty of care towards young people. However, this certainly does not mean 'wrapping them in cotton wool'. Therefore, we have responsibility not only to keep young people safe, but also to enable them to learn to manage risks for themselves.* (LOTC, 2018) "

There are three things that should be considered when deciding whether a risk is acceptable: (Ball et al., 2008, p. 114)

1. likelihood of children coming to harm
2. severity of that harm
3. benefits, rewards or outcomes of that activity for the children.

Some risk assessment considerations

In the following sections, we gather together specific advice about how to manage some common risks when teaching outdoors.

Behaviour and safeguarding

The outdoor learning policy should reflect the school health and safety and behaviour policies. Whilst the outdoors can provide an exciting and stimulating environment, it is always important to provide clear expectations of behaviour, with consistent consequence systems to ensure safe practice. Positive reinforcement through effective communication and engagement should always be demonstrated. Children should be encouraged to understand what unacceptable behaviour is, with incidents recorded in line with school policy where appropriate.

Where unacceptable behaviour occurs and an oral reprimand has been given, the more informal atmosphere outside the classroom often provides time and opportunity to discuss possible consequences of such behaviour, such as the potential harm caused and loss of privileges, e.g. use of tools or lighting fires. It may also provide space to discuss feelings and emotions underlying the inappropriate behaviour (Hopper, 2017). However, where the child is at serious risk of hurting themselves or others and likely to suffer or inflict significant harm, the child should be removed from the context, following school procedures in line with the school's safeguarding policy (DfE, 2018b).

First aid

Injuries are not very common when safe practices are adopted and children have been involved in discussions about what needs to be done to keep everyone safe in the outdoor area and why. When delivering outdoor activities, it is important to adhere to your setting practice and policy. With reference to first aid, it is often recommended that the lead practitioner holds an up-to-date recognised first aid qualification. If not, they must have a working knowledge of first aid appropriate to the activities that they are leading and the location in which they are working. They must also have immediate access to a qualified first aider in the event of needing further support. The general school policy about administering or securing first aid should always be followed (Hammett, 2016; DfE, 2018b). When working in areas where there is a risk of ticks, long-sleeved tops and trousers tucked into socks should be worn and parents alerted to check their children for ticks after school.

If working away from site, or more than ten minutes from immediate help, we strongly recommend attending a two-day emergency first aid in the outdoors course (such as one offered by BASP UK), which covers remote first aid practices and procedures and will give additional confidence in managing potential hazards.

Fire-lighting, cooking and use of tools

To support you with the activities in this book, we have put together some step-by-step principles for the safe use of tools, the teaching of fire-lighting and cooking in the outdoors, and the use of a storm kettle. The step-by-step principle has been used to support children in developing key skills and breaking these skills down into key components, which they can then apply to the task. These have been adapted from the Wild Tribe Outdoor Learning programme (2019).

Fire-lighting and safe practice

Fire can be hazardous and dangerous when not managed effectively. It can have a devastating impact on the environment and natural landscapes if it gets out of control. However, children find fire exciting and, if the skills of fire-lighting are taught with safety as a prerequisite, lessons that include fire will ignite children's imaginations.

Fire safety advice

- Provide adequate supervision for young people when using fires and ensure that they have been taught the appropriate skills to make a fire.
- Avoid making fires on stones or near tree roots.
- Monitor weather conditions and changes in wind direction. A strong wind could contribute to a fire becoming out of control.
- Do not light fires in excessively dry conditions.
- Place all equipment, including fuel, in safe boxes.
- Never leave a fire unattended.
- Keep wood and other fuel sources away from fire.

- Have a supply of water available to extinguish the fire and to remedy burns.
- Do not underestimate the power of fire.
- Thoroughly extinguish all fires.
- Leave no trace (for more information, see: lnt.org/why/7-principles/minimize-campfire-impacts).

Lighting fires: safe preparation, lighting and management

Equipment:

- matches or fire strikers
- water
- wood of various thicknesses: about 15–20 cm (6–8 inches) long
- tinder, such as dried leaves, birch bark or cotton wool balls
- petroleum jelly, e.g. Vaseline®.

Preparation:

1. Identify the area to be used as a group fire-lighting area (the main area) and surround this with well-defined markers such as large branches or tree stump seats.
2. Place four sticks of wrist-thickness in a square in the middle to denote a safety area, about 45 cm (18 inches) square.
3. Collect fuel for the fire. If the weather has been wet, collect sticks for the fire a few days prior to the session and allow them to dry out. You can then scatter these dry twigs in the area for the children to 'find'. As an alternative, a bag of bought kindling can also be used.
4. Keep a selection of dried sticks of varying widths – pencil, finger, thumb and wrist width – in a bag near the fire circle for teacher use.
5. Seated around the prepared area, talk to children about safety aspects of fires, emphasising safe practice around a fire.
   a. Hair needs to be tied back. Hair contains high levels of oil, which is highly flammable.
   b. Appropriate clothing (long sleeves and long trousers) should be worn.
   c. Responsible behaviour will negate risk to self or others.
   d. No one to enter the inner fire square unless invited to do so.
   e. If invited, adopt the safe stance: kneeling on one knee and one foot on the ground.
   f. Point out the container of water placed near the fire area used to extinguish the flames.

Step-by-step method

Introduce the 'fire triangle theory', i.e. that fires need three things – heat, fuel and oxygen.

Show children how to light a fire using a step-by-step method:

1. Choose a suitable site. This could be a flat or sloped area, grass covered or bare ground.

2. Clear the area of loose vegetation and stones. **See A**

3. Show the children how to make a platform of about four or five sticks on which to build a fire to keep it off the damp floor and provide oxygen (draught). **See B**

4. In groups, ask the children to:
   a. Find a good area for the fire.
   b. Clear the area from vegetation and stones.
   c. Find four sticks to mark a safe area in which to build the fire.
   d. Find four or five sticks to put as a platform on which to build the fire.

5. Once groups have achieved this, bring them back to the main area and explain that now they need fuel for the fire.

6. Show the children the prepared selection of sticks and group them according to width – pencil, finger and thumb. **See C**

7. Ask the children to suggest why this has been done. Explain that when the fire is lit, the smallest sticks will be used as fuel first, before gradually adding the larger sticks.

8. Ask the children to collect a selection of sticks with different widths. Explain that they need to be able to 'snap', as this shows that they are dry and able to burn.

9. The children now order their sticks by thickness.

10. Explain that the next step is how a fire should be laid – would just throwing the sticks in a pile work or would they suggest arranging them in some way? Do we need anything that will light easily to put on first?

11. Demonstrate how to place pulled cotton wool and petroleum jelly or a straw sphere on the prepared platform.

12. Show how to add the tinder, building the fire base up using the thinnest pencil sticks first, ensuring that there is enough air between the sticks. **See D**

13. What else do we need for our fire in case we need to stop it? Ensure that there is a container of water next to the demonstration fire.

14. Revise talk of safety around the fire: the safety stance.

15. Demonstrate how to ignite the kindling using a long match or fire strikers, reinforcing the safety stance.

16. Children return to their prepared bases to lay their fires, each group checking that they have a bottle of water to place next to their prepared areas.

17. Once the adult with the group is happy with the laying of the fire, they should supervise the lighting of it.

18. The children must sit down once the fire is lit and be supervised at all times.

19. Children can put more wood on, one piece at a time, when needed, but must not lean across the fire to do so.

NEVER LEAVE THE FIRE UNATTENDED.

Key steps for using a storm kettle

The storm kettle looks hollow (which acts as a chimney) but has an internal chamber for water, which is not obvious. Take the time to show the storm kettle to the children and ask them how they think it works.

The main differences to consider when using a storm kettle compared to lighting a fire are:

1. Clearing a base – this needs to be a very level site so that the storm kettle doesn't fall over.

2. The fire is built in the storm kettle base, so although pencil, finger and thumb sticks still need collecting, the length of them needs to be quite short to fit into the base, like this: **See A**

3. When putting the storm kettle on and taking it off the base, keep the handle horizontal so that fingers are not over the hot chimney, to avoid burns. The safe method looks like this: **See B**

Your setting may also recommend the use of heat-resistant gloves.

4. Once the kettle is on the base, the fire is fed through the chimney.

   a. Short sticks should be put onto the rim and tipped into the chimney.

   b. At no point should fingers go across the chimney.

5. When the water is boiled and the kettle lifted off, the water should be poured into cups using the handle and the cork. **See C**

6. Cups should be put onto a flat surface or held by an adult when the water is being poured. The children must not hold them until they have cooled.

7. Once the storm kettle is cool, you should remove any remaining water and then empty any remaining embers from the base of the kettle.

8. You should then follow the principles below for extinguishing fires to deal with the remaining embers. **See D**

9. Once the storm kettle is cool, it can be safely stored by turning the base upside down and inserting it inside the bottom of the storm kettle, before placing the kettle in its bag.

Extinguishing fires – leaving minimal trace

1. Once all the cooking has been completed and it is time for the fire to be put out, choose a responsible child to slowly pour a bottle of water over the fire.

2. Make sure they demonstrate the safe stance, kneeling with one knee up.

3. Check that the white ash from the wood, which is the hottest part, has been covered with water, and that the fire is properly out.

4. With a stick that has not been used on the fire, ask the children to scrape the embers around so that no remains of the fire can be seen, and that the area is left as it was found.

If it is a permanent fire area on the site, the remaining charcoal can be left.

As the children become more experienced and proficient and are able to demonstrate safe practice, they can become more independent; however, strict adult vigilance should be observed at all times.

Using tools – principles and practices

Children should be taught how to use tools safely and with respect. We recommend the following general safe practice under close adult supervision (Outdoor and Woodland Learning, 2017):

- Ensure that the tools are appropriate and suit the purpose.

- Keep tools in a safe place (e.g. a locked cabinet) and ensure they are well maintained.

- Ensure that tools are counted out at the beginning and counted back in at the end of a session.

- Mark tools with coloured tape so they are easy to spot, especially if they are green or black.

- During a session tools should be kept in a marked-off area and children should only access them when they are given permission, with adult supervision.

- Ratios for tool use should initially be one to one and no more than six to eight per adult once children have been trained and are confident in using them safely.

- Children should position themselves in a safe space prior to using any tools. They should not be able to make contact with another child when they stretch out their arms.

Using a bow saw

1. Show the children the parts of the saw: handle, blade, and cover.

2. Remove the cover and show the cutting edge.

3. Show how to hold the saw using the handle with the blade pointing down.

4. Working in pairs, one child or adult should hold the piece of wood to stop it from moving. The other places their hand through the handle of the bow saw so that their sawing hand is well away from the cutting edge, as shown.

5. When the saw is not in use, it should be placed with the blade facing in and down.

Using a folding saw to cut small pieces of wood

1. Show the children the parts of the saw: handle, button to release the blade and cutting edge.

2. Show how to use the button to release the cutting edge.

3. Show how to hold the saw. The free hand goes over the saw and holds the material.

4. Work in pairs. Push forwards and pull backwards with the blade pointing downwards.

5. After using the saw, show how to press and pinch to close the blade. When passing the saw, it should be face downward with the blade closed.

Using a bill hook to split wood (under close supervision)

1. Show the children the parts of the bill hook: handle, blade and cutting edge.

2. Show them that their free hand should be placed behind their back when they are using the bill hook.

3. Demonstrate using the blade away from the body, hook facing downwards, keeping the blade parallel and close to the wood.

4. Always carry the tool by the handle with the blade facing downwards.

5. Adults should replace the cover on the blade after use.

Using a sheath knife

1. Show the children the parts of the knife: handle, sheath (cover), blade and cutting edge.

2. Show how to remove the sheath safely.

3. Demonstrate how to assume a bent knee position with the knife away from the body and move the knife downwards and away.

4. When not in use, the knife should be placed in its sheath.

5. Show how to pass the knife with the sheath pointing downwards.

Using secateurs to cut twigs (diameter smaller than 1p coin)

1. Show the children the parts of the secateurs: handle and blades.

2. Show how to release the blades and show the cutting edge.

3. Explain that your free hand holds the item you are cutting, like when using a big pair of scissors.

4. To pass the secateurs, children must close the blades and pass them using the handle with the blades pointing downwards.

5. When not in use the blades should be securely closed.

Using loppers to cut branches (diameter smaller than 2p coin)

1. Show the children the parts of the lopper: handle, blade and cutting edge.

2. Show them how to hold the loppers with two hands.

3. Demonstrate how to pass the loppers, with blades pointing down.

4. Show the children how to cut the wood in pairs, like this:

5. When not in use, the loppers should be placed down with the blades facing towards the back of the child.

6. Show how to carry them pointing downwards.

Drilling

Drilling stumps are useful: they help children keep the wood still and provide a safe space.

Using a palm drill to make small holes in wood and remove pith

1. Show the children the parts of a drill: handle and drill bit.

2. Use the drill with one hand and twist and push down.

3. When removing the drill bit pull it up and out.

4. Show how to point the drill bit down and pass with the handle to another person.

5. Replace the drill in the toolbox after use.

Using a hand drill to make larger holes in wood

1. Show the children the parts of the drill: handle, bit holder and drill bit.

2. Show how to turn the bit holder to open it to insert the drill bit.

3. Turn the bit holder the opposite way to close the bit holder.

4. The children will need to use two hands, one hand holding the drill and one hand turning the drill bit.

5. Children should pass the drill by holding the handle with the drill bit facing down or removed.

6. Replace the drill in the toolbox after use.

Accepting challenge and staying safe

Practitioners are advised to attend training courses and practise before delivering a session with children. Attending a training course will advance your own skills, and ensure you are delivering high quality safe sessions. Health and safety considerations are positive aspects of teaching outdoors rather than barriers since they enable children to take risks in a safe and secure risk-assessed environment. Through experiencing challenges, children develop the capability to weigh up situations and take appropriate action. This is a vital life skill that schools can foster by providing proportionate responses to any identified health and safety issues.

English

In this unit, children will be focusing on the development of their writing skills. Based on the Key Stage 2 English objectives identified in the 2014 National Curriculum for England, the children will be introduced to a sense of place through their five senses. They will explore the outdoor learning area using each of the senses and use this experience as a catalyst to ignite their writing. Children will be given the opportunity to develop poetry, stories and non-fiction writing as they establish a personal and reflective sense of place.

To support inclusive practice or to extend learning, the space, task, equipment and people (STEP) approach can be adopted throughout this unit. By changing the space, task, equipment or people, the activity can be made more challenging or easier to understand, enabling all pupils to take part in the activity, as explained in the assessment chapter in this book.

The children will be expected to work as a whole class directed by the teacher, together in pairs or small groups with support from adults, and independently.

The role of the adult is to lead the sessions safely, modelling the activities, allowing experimentation and independence whilst providing direct support.

You may wish to record the activities using a camera.

Natural connections

- Enhanced awareness of local natural environments and changes within them

- Observation skills, looking at characters created by natural materials.

Health and wellbeing

- Physical activity

- Being focused and attentive

- Teambuilding activities

- Emotional resilience and independent learning.

Word bank

Senses

- sight
- sound
- touch
- hearing

- place
- values
- themes
- sensory

English

- haiku poetry
- descriptive language
- composition
- non-fiction
- fiction
- comprehension

- syllables
- rhythm
- structure
- kennings poetry
- interactive guide

Summary overview

Progression	Curriculum content	Learning experiences/activities
Lesson 1	Draft and write by composing and rehearsing sentences orally, progressively building a varied and rich vocabulary and an increasing range of sentence structures.	Children will begin to develop a sense of place through sight. They will ask questions to develop their sense of place. They will build a rich vocabulary to describe the look of the outdoor setting. They will use clay to create a tree monster and use descriptive language to develop the character they have made.
Lesson 2	Listen to and discuss a wide range of poetry. Prepare poems to read aloud and to perform, showing understanding through intonation, tone, volume and action.	Children will explore their sense of place through sound. They will record sounds they can hear and use these to develop a haiku poem to read to a partner. They will make rhythm sticks to support their performance.
Lesson 3	Retrieve and record information from non-fiction books and articles. Draft and write narratives, creating settings, characters and plots.	Children will use their sense of smell to explore the outdoor area. Children will make their own 'smelly potion', using this as a stimulus to create a setting and a plot for a story.
Lesson 4	Retrieve and record information from non-fiction books and articles. Identify how language, structure and presentation contribute to meaning.	Children will experience foraging. They will identify the plants and fruits that are edible. They will retrieve recipes and information about plants from non-fiction sources. They will look at how recipes are structured and how to follow them to make some foraged dishes.
Lesson 5	Listen to and discuss a wide range of poetry. Prepare poems to read aloud and to perform, showing understanding through intonation, tone, volume and action.	Children will develop their own kennings poetry in this session, using the sense of touch. They will explore the outdoor space through touch and develop an interactive sensory stick to describe the outdoor place. They will read and discuss kennings poetry and perform poetry through intonation, tone, volume and action.
Lesson 6	Listen to and discuss a wide range of poetry. Prepare poems to read aloud and to perform, showing understanding through intonation, tone, volume and action. Retrieve and record information from non-fiction books and articles.	In this final lesson, the children will consider all five senses and how they have developed a sense of the outdoor place. The children will develop a sensory memory structure. They will research what is needed to make a sensory garden and prepare sensory poems to read aloud. They will prepare a sensory celebration about the outdoor place.

PREPARATION

Ensure that children have access to a safe outdoor area where they can explore a sense of place through the sense of sight and record their observations.

Review this Cornwall County Council unit about how the locality can inform a sense of place: www.sense-of-place. co.uk/preview/docs/Our%20 Special%20Place-%20unit.pdf

Resources

- Mirrors
- Adjectives cards (cards with adjectives written on them, such as 'golden', 'reflective' or 'bright')
- Clay
- Whiteboards
- Pens
- Images of 'tree faces' ('faces' that can be seen in the features of trees or faces that have been created on trees using clay)
- Fire-making kit

CONSIDER

Health & Safety

Assess and evaluate hazards and risks in your setting. See the health and safety chapter.

LESSON OBJECTIVES

We are developing a sense of place through the sense of sight.

We are creating a tree monster and developing a character that can be described using descriptive language.

National Curriculum Content

- Draft and write by composing and rehearsing sentences orally, progressively building a varied and rich vocabulary and an increasing range of sentence structures.

ADULT ROLES

- Support the children in finding and describing a range of objects to match their adjective.
- Encourage the children to use descriptive language to describe the clay character they have created.

WARM UP IDEAS

Squirrel climb (individual)

Encourage the children to hold a mirror reflective side-up, with one edge against the bridge of their nose so they can see into the mirror. Tell them to choose a tree in the outdoor area. By looking in their mirrors, children do a 'squirrel climb' up the tree and note the view. They then describe this view to a partner. Ask them to choose another tree and repeat the squirrel climb. What can they see? How different does this tree look through the mirror? How would they describe this viewpoint?

Introductory activity

Talk to the children about the outdoor learning area and ask them to describe the place where they are. Answer key questions like:

- Where would you go to be alone?
- Which tree would you like to climb?
- What is the most beautiful thing you have ever seen in the area?
- If you could take one thing with you from this place, what would it be?
- What colours can you see?
- How do you feel? Do you feel safe/excited/calm/happy?

See the preparation section for further sense of place ideas and additional questions.

MAIN ACTIVITIES

Sense of place: sight

Challenge 1 (individual and in pairs)

Adjectives game

Give each child a card with an adjective written on it, e.g. golden, reflective, etc. Ask them to collect as many natural and man-made objects linked to that adjective as they can in ten minutes. Discuss with a partner:

- What items have they found that match the adjective?
- Can they use the adjective to construct some descriptive sentences about the objects they have found?
- Can they use other adjectives to describe the objects and the place in which they found them?

Challenge 2 (whole class, individual and in pairs)

Tree monsters

Discuss any natural faces that children can spot in the outdoor learning area.

- Can they see faces within the trees?
- Do the trees create shadows that also create faces?
- Can they find any other places where natural faces are created?
- Show the children some images of tree monsters created using the natural features of the trees and natural objects.
- Give each child some clay and ask them to create tree monsters using existing tree features.

Once the clay characters have been made, pairs discuss:

- What is the name of your tree character?
- What special powers do they have?
- Where have they come from?
- Where do they live?
- Why are they in this place?

Challenge 3 (groups of four)

Character tree walk

Encourage groups to look at all the tree monsters and characters that have been created in the area. How have they used the natural features of trees and plants to create the tree faces? How would they describe some of the characters they have seen? Ask them to list words on a whiteboard to describe the different characters.

Extension (whole class and in pairs)

Tree monster tales

If there is time, build a fire using the step-by-step principles from the health and safety chapter. Encourage the children to talk about their tree monsters and use them to tell a partner a story involving their character, using the questions previously discussed as a framework.

PLENARY

Talk to the children about what they have seen and observed in the outdoor area. What natural objects have they found? What natural objects and features did they use to make their clay faces/tree monsters? How would they describe the outdoor space based on what they can see? Refer back to the sense of place questions in the introductory activity.

Back in the classroom

- Write a description of the tree character they have made.
- Write a description of the outdoor learning area and the natural faces that they have found in this area.
- Develop a whole-class interactive guide to the outdoor learning area, starting with what they can see in the area, and develop a section on a sense of the outdoor place through sight.
- Encourage the children to write sentences to describe their outdoor space by writing on a 'sight postcard', which could be given to someone who has never been to the area or be used for a display.

EVALUATION/FOLLOW ON

- What went well today?
- Which children understood the concepts?
- Which children needed more help?
- Are there other resources you can use?
- Can you use some the sense of sight postcards to develop a sense of place display in the classroom?

PREPARATION

Ensure that you have access to an outdoor area where the children are able to listen to and record a variety of sounds.

Review www.primaryresources.co.uk/english/powerpoints/Haiku_Poems.ppt. Print some examples.

Forest Craft by Richard Irvine provides further ideas for the development of a rhythm stick.

Resources

- Sound poems, tablet and blank postcards
- Mallets, sheaf knives and hazel sticks
- Tin cans
- Double-sided tape
- Examples of haikus

Previous learning

Talk to the children about what a sense of place means and revisit some of the sense of place questions from the first lesson.

CONSIDER

Health & Safety

Assess and evaluate hazards and risks in your setting. See the health and safety chapter.

LESSON OBJECTIVES

We are developing a sense of place through sound. We are identifying sounds and developing a haiku poem using the sounds of the outdoor place.

National Curriculum Content

- Listen to and discuss a wide range of poetry.
- Prepare poems to read aloud and to perform, showing understanding through intonation, tone, volume and action.

ADULT ROLES

- Support the children in developing a haiku poem.
- Encourage the children to use language that supports rhythm.

WARM UP IDEAS

Human camera (in pairs)

Tell the children to lead their partner, who has their eyes closed, to a nice view in the outdoor area. Remind them that they need to ask their partner's permission to gently touch their ear and say 'Click!', so that their partner opens their eyes and can take in the view like a snapshot. Swap roles. Repeat this activity three times. Encourage the children to remember as much as they can about their favourite view and draw their view on a postcard, using descriptive language to describe it on the other side.

Introductory activity (individual and whole class)

Magic spot

Ask the children to find their own space, which is their 'magic spot'. This could be in a secret den, under a tree or sitting beside their favourite log. Explain that this is a reflective activity, where they need to sit on their magic spot and listen carefully to what they can hear.

Key questions to ask the children before and as a result of the activity:

- Can they hear the leaves in the outdoor area?
- What was the loudest sound they heard?
- What was the quietest sound they heard?
- What sounds can they hear that sum up this place well?

MAIN ACTIVITIES

Sense of place: sound

Challenge 1 (individual and in pairs)

Magic spot sounds

Returning to their magic spot or a new place, children record all the sounds they can hear in words and pictures on a postcard.

Looking at the words on their postcard, can they work out how many syllables the word has? For example, rustling has two.

Encourage the children to tap out the words on their knees if they are unsure about how many syllables the word has.

When they have completed this task, encourage pairs to share the words and pictures they have recorded on the postcards. Check that the number of syllables recorded is correct for the words listed. Are there any tricky words they have identified where there is a disagreement on the number of syllables?

Note: local dialect may influence the number of syllables children identify in some words.

Challenge 2 (individual and in pairs)

Haikus

Show the children some examples of a haiku poem. Read some haiku poems relating to the outdoors to the children. Can they use their sound postcards to develop a haiku poem? Remind the children that they need five syllables in the first line, seven in the second line and five in the final line.

Once the children have developed their poems, encourage them to read them to a partner, ensuring that the 5, 7, 5 pattern has been followed. What descriptive words give a real sense of the sounds?

Challenge 3 Extension (individual)

Natural instruments

If there is time, let children select natural objects to make a musical instrument. This could be a simple instrument made using a clean tin can with natural objects inside to make a shaker. Double-sided sticky tape could be placed around the outside to decorate the instrument. Other instruments could include a rhythm stick, which could be created using a sheath knife and mallet following the instructions below. Following the guidance in the health and safety chapter for safe knife use, work individually.

- The knife is placed on a hazel stick and a mallet is used to tap the knife to score the wood.

- Then whittle a mark in the wood using the knife.

- This is repeated several times down the stick to create an undulating effect on the stick.

- Can they make instruments that reproduce some of the natural sounds that they hear in this place?

PLENARY

Discuss with the children the sounds they have heard in the outdoor area. What have they learned about haiku poetry and the use of words to form a haiku poem? What musical instruments have they developed and how has this helped them to perform poetry?

Back in the classroom

- Develop a class book of haiku poems.

- Continue to develop the whole-class interactive guide to the outdoor area; include a haiku poetry and sounds section within the guide.

- Continue to develop sounds that reflect and describe the outdoor learning area.

- Create and perform a whole-class rhythm poem about the soundscape, using the natural instruments to play music that evokes the sense of place.

EVALUATION/FOLLOW ON

- What went well today?

- Which children understood the concepts?

- Which children needed more help?

- Are there other resources you can use?

- Can you use some of the instruments made to make a display of different materials in the classroom?

PREPARATION

Ensure that the children have access to a safe outdoor area where they will be able to experience and record a range of smells.

Review www.gardeningknowhow.com/special/children/herb-gardens-for-children.htm

Resources

- Range of herbs and other items with distinctive smells, placed in bowls/plates
- Pine cones, paper cups, water and food colouring
- Tiles, safety glasses and gloves, mallets and outdoor tile grout
- Plant pots and compost
- Cloth and wet wipes
- Herbs or seeds for planting a pizza garden: oregano, parsley and basil
- Story prompt cards

Previous learning

Talk to the children about the sense of place through sight and sound; what have they discovered so far?

CONSIDER

Health & Safety

Assess and evaluate hazards and risks in your setting. See the health and safety chapter.

LESSON OBJECTIVES

We are exploring a sense of place through smell. We are making smelly potions and using them to create a setting and a plot for a story.

National Curriculum Content

- Retrieve and record information from non-fiction books and articles.
- Draft and write narratives, creating settings, characters and plots.

ADULT ROLES

- Support the children in finding a plant that smells and encourage the children to develop a narrative, using the smelly cocktail as part of the plot.

WARM UP IDEAS

Whole class

Children stand in a circle. Explain that you will throw the pine cone to someone in a circle and call out earth, water or sky as you throw. The child receiving the pine cone must name an animal that lives in the earth, water or sky, whichever has been called. They then throw the cone to another person, calling out either earth, water or sky and the child that catches the cone has to name another animal, and so on. If a child struggles to name one, the children on either side of them can help.

Introductory activity (whole class and in pairs)

Discuss what the children have learned to date about the outdoor learning area. What have they seen and heard? How have they recorded these observations and used them to develop their descriptive writing? What have they learned about this place in particular? In this lesson, the children will focus on smell. What smells can they already detect in the outdoor area?

Have a range of different plants and other items that the children can smell placed in pots and small bowls. In pairs, one child closes their eyes and the other selects a plant/plate for the other child to guess the smell.

- Can they identify any smells?
- What words can they use to describe the different odours?
- What herbs do they know?
- Do they know what the herbs are used for?
- How easy or hard is it to use only the sense of smell to identify plants?

MAIN ACTIVITIES

Sense of place: smell

Challenge 1 (individual)

Smelly potion

Give each child a reusable paper cup and explain that they need to find as many things as they can in the outdoor area to make a smelly woodland potion, as well as a stick to stir it with. Go through some key safety principles with the children about what plants and objects they are not permitted to touch to ensure safety. When the children have collected their items, they fill the cup with coloured water and sprinkle it with 'magic dust'.

- Ask the children to think of a name for their smelly potion.

- What special powers does it have?

- Can they describe the colour, texture and smell?

- How does their woodland potion reflect the place where it was found?

Challenge 2 (in pairs)

Potion tales

Ask the children to think of a plot for a story involving their smelly potion. Model an example with the children, using a story prompt card to support the storytelling. The card could have symbols and pictures on it to support the storytelling process. For example:

- Two children were playing in the woods on a sunny afternoon. They were mixing potions when, with a stir of a stick, they suddenly disappeared in a puff of purple smoke.

- Where did they go?

- Who did they see?

- What was their quest?

- How did they return?

Pairs begin to devise a tale.

Challenge 3 (in pairs)

Mini herb garden

Each pair has a plant pot.

- If deemed safe, let the children use a mallet, wearing safety gloves and glasses, to break up some tiles.

- Still wearing gloves to handle the tiles and outdoor tile grout, place the small broken tiles on the plant pot covered in tile cement in a mosaic design. Once the design is in place, spread tile grout over the tiles to seal the design.

- Clean the tiles immediately, using a wet wipe or damp cloth to clean the design before allowing it to dry.

- Once the pot has been completed, children can fill the pot with compost.

- They can make a pizza herb garden by planting basil, parsley and oregano, either as seeds or as seedlings.

PLENARY

Discuss with the children the smells they have experienced in the outdoor area. What have they planted in their mini herb gardens? How can they use the smelly woodland potion they have developed to support them in story-writing?

Back in the classroom

- Use the smelly potion and its magic powers and develop these names and ideas into a story.

- Build on the interactive guide to the outdoor learning area so that it includes an interactive guide to smells and the herb gardens that have been developed.

EVALUATION/FOLLOW ON

- What went well today?

- Which children understood the concepts?

- Which children needed more help?

- Are there other resources you can use?

- Can you use some of the plants or natural objects collected to make a display of different smells in the classroom?

PREPARATION

Ensure that the children have access to a range of items that they could taste. These can be brought in if they do not grow naturally in the outdoor area but ensure that you have the leaves or source of the items to show the children, to help them with identification of the plant or tree, e.g. if bringing in blackberries, show the children the plant these come from.

Identify any harmful plants and fruits and make these known to the children by marking them with a red cone or label.

Resources

- Food items, blindfolds and tray
- Sets of images of non-edible and edible plants, flowers and fruits
- Pens to write on leaves
- https://naturedetectives. woodlandtrust.org. uk/naturedetectives/ activities/2015/06/fantastic-fruits-and-seeds
- https://naturedetectives. woodlandtrust.org.uk/ naturedetectives/blogs/ nature-detectives-blog/2016/09/autumn-foraging-tips-kids
- Fire-making kit
- Folded flatbreads, cheese, tomato puree, foil, griddle, pan and herbs.
- Ingredients for dandelion recipes: www. ediblewildfood.com/ dandelion-fritters.aspx

Previous learning

Talk to the children about the sense of place through sight, sound and smell; what have they discovered so far?

LESSON OBJECTIVES

We are developing a sense of place through taste and foraging for natural food items. We are following written recipes and looking at how they are structured.

National Curriculum Content

- Retrieve and record information from non-fiction books and articles.
- Identify how language, structure and presentation contribute to meaning.

ADULT ROLES

- Support the children in finding items in the outdoor area that are edible.
- Support them in using recipes and with how to follow the structure.

WARM UP IDEAS

In pairs

Place a range of natural food items on a tray. One child is blindfolded/closes their eyes and the other takes a food item for them to guess what it is. They then swap. Do they guess the natural food items correctly?

Introductory activity (whole class)

Explain that this week children are going to develop a sense of place through taste. What do they know about foraging? What does this mean?

They will be able to forage for items that they can eat within the outdoor area but must only eat them if they have checked safety with an adult. Give groups a range of pictures of fruit, flowers, plants and trees and some actual plants to look for. Tell them that they will be sorting items that they collect into edible and non-edible foods later.

Note: If you are foraging for the first time with children, ensure that you only ask them to look for items where there is no doubt as to what the flower or plant is, e.g. dandelions, primroses, etc. Always emphasise that children should only taste them if they have checked with an adult.

CONSIDER

Health & Safety

Assess and evaluate hazards and risks in your setting. See the health and safety chapter.

MAIN ACTIVITIES

Sense of place: taste

Challenge 1 (groups of four and whole class)

Foraging

Using their guides, groups 'forage' in the area for plants and fruits. Explain that first they will be just identifying them and sorting them into items that are edible and those that are not.

- Can they find any of the items they have identified in the introductory activity? Have they found any new items?
- Use the identification cards to identify any items they are not sure about.

After an adult has checked them for safety, children can try some plants and fruits.

- What tastes are there in this place?
- What are your favourite tastes?
- How can you use the taste to develop an autumnal delight dish? Can we use the herb garden created in the previous session?
- Ask children to collect leaves to write on – they write down the tastes that are in the outdoor area, one per leaf.
- Select a branch and hang the leaves on a branch to make a taste tree. You could include the leaves of herbs, such as mint. Draw attention to the link between smells and tastes.

Challenge 2 (groups of four)

Recipes and instructional writing

Show children a range of recipes that can be made from foraged foods. Draw attention to how the text is structured and how this helps the reader to follow the recipe instructions to make a dish.

- Give groups the opportunity to choose a recipe that they could make from the foods they have foraged, e.g. dandelion fritters.
- Groups then select and prepare the ingredients for a recipe. If heat is required for the recipe, follow the step-by-step principles for fire-making.

Challenge 3 (individual)

Extension – pizzas

If there is time, use the step-by-step principles of fire-making, in the health and safety chapter, so that children can make their own pizza. Children select a folded flatbread. Place tomato puree on one side of the bread and then sprinkle cheese on top. Place the flatbread in foil and fold the foil around the flatbread. Use tongs to place the pizza in the embers of the fire to cook. Once cooked, the pizza could be served with the pizza herbs from Progression 3 – oregano, basil and parsley – chopped into fine pieces. Note: Herbs may need to be bought if the herb garden was planted as seeds. Encourage pairs to describe the tastes and how they might describe the pizza on a menu.

PLENARY

Discuss with the children the tastes they have experienced in the outdoor area. Which herbs in the mini herb gardens have a strong flavour? How can they use the tastes that are in their outdoor area to develop their own 'sense of taste' recipe book? What new descriptive words have they used?

Back in the classroom

- Continue to develop the interactive guide to the outdoor area and record the tastes in the area.
- Create a class forage recipe book that includes use of items that can be foraged for in the outdoor area and herbs from the herb garden. This could be entitled 'Autumnal Delights'.

EVALUATION/FOLLOW ON

- What went well today?
- Which children understood the concepts?
- Which children needed more help?
- Are there other resources you can use?
- Can you use the taste tree to inspire a collection of outdoor tastes that could be on display in the classroom?

PREPARATION

Ensure that the children have access to a range of items that they can touch and which grow naturally in the area. Check for harmful objects.

Place some items in the area that would not normally be found there to provide a range of different textures if necessary.

Review www.twinkl.co.uk/resource/t2-e-1009-recognise-some-different-forms-of-kennings-kennings-lesson-teaching-pack.

Resources

- Examples of kennings poems
- Brightly coloured sticky notes for markers
- String
- Pegs
- Small natural bags
- Range of natural items
- Whiteboards
- Pens

Previous learning

Talk to the children about the sense of place through sight, sound, smell and touch. What have they discovered so far?

CONSIDER

Health & Safety

Assess and evaluate hazards and risks in your setting. See the health and safety chapter.

LESSON OBJECTIVES

We are developing a sense of place through touch. We are developing an understanding of kennings poetry.

National Curriculum Content

- Listen to and discuss a wide range of poetry.
- Prepare poems to read aloud and to perform, showing understanding through intonation, tone, volume and action.

ADULT ROLES

- Support the children in finding and describing a range of natural objects to touch.
- Encourage the children to use descriptive language to develop a kennings poem.

WARM UP IDEAS

Explore the area together through the sense of touch. Let children remove or place a marker by any items that are not usually in the place, ensuring that the children do not pick up any harmful objects. Discuss safety, such as the use of litter pickers or gloves if items are sharp or if you do not want them to touch any objects. Ask children to consider:

- What materials make up this place?
- How could they describe this place to someone who cannot see but can only touch?
- What would they give them to hold, so that they can get a sense of the place through touch?
- What items best describe this place through touch?
- What descriptive words could they use to say what objects feel like?

Introductory activity (in pairs)

Pairs create a trail by pegging natural objects found in the outdoor learning area to a piece of string. Once they have made their natural trail, with their eyes closed they swap them with another pair and try to identify the items on the string.

Sense of place: touch

Challenge 1 (in pairs)

Who am I?

One child in the pair puts a blindfold on. All the children who are blindfolded then sit together in a safe space. You then direct the remaining children to sit in front of another child not from their original pair. The child who is blindfolded can ask the child in front of them a range of questions, except their name. They must guess who is in front of them. The child not blindfolded may need to disguise their voice. The children can then swap over to play the game again.

Challenge 2 (whole class, individual and in pairs)

Kennings poetry development

Talk to the children about the game and how they had to ask a range of questions to guess who was in front of them. Explain that kennings poems are very short 'who am I' poems that give clues like a riddle by describing characteristics of the person or object. Give the children an example of a kennings poem.

- Sweet-tasting
- Nitrogen-fixing
- Four-leaved
- Lucky plant
- Who am I?
- Answer: Clover

Further examples can be found in the preparation section.

Give each child a small bag and ask them to go and find a secret natural item to place in the bag. They pick an item that their partner will try to guess. Once they have found an item, pairs will need to take it in turns to ask each other questions about what is in their bag and try to guess the item. Can they now use some of the questions to develop their own kennings poem about the item? For example:

- Small dome
- Spirals circle
- Hard shell
- Animal home
- Who am I?
- Answer: Snail shell

Encourage the children to build the poem using two words in each line, and for the clues to the object to get easier throughout the poem. They can record these using a whiteboard and pen or find a natural item to write on such as bark. Can they perform their poems to the rest of the class? How can they use tone in their poem? Can they vary the volume? Can they put any actions in place?

Challenge 3 (individual)

Woodland guide by touch

Encourage the children to collect items to develop a woodland guide to this place through a sense of touch. How could you sum up this place by things you can touch? Ask the children to develop a sensory stick using a range of materials to describe the outdoor place through touch.

Discuss what the children have found out about this place through a sense of touch. How can they use their kennings poems to develop their poetry writing?

Back in the classroom

- Create an interactive guide through the use of touch about the outside space, for use by someone who is partially sighted.
- Develop a class book of kennings poems.
- Record kennings poetry in the outdoor area to share with other classes.
- Use the metaphors developed in their kennings for writing other forms of poetry or prose.

- What went well today?
- Which children understood the concepts?
- Which children needed more help?
- Are there other resources you can use?
- Can you use some of the materials collected to make a display of different materials that describe the place through a sense of touch, e.g. sensory sticks?

PREPARATION

Ensure that children have access to a safe outdoor area where they can explore a sense of place through all five senses.

Review https://schoolgardening.rhs.org.uk/resources/info-sheet/setting-up-a-school-garden and www.sensorytrust.org.uk/information/factsheets/sensory-garden-1.html.

Resources

- Pens
- A branch and craft items to develop a sensory memory sculpture
- Plants, compost garden tools and seeds to develop a sensory garden
- Written work that the children have completed from previous sessions
- Ingredients for 'Autumnal Delights' recipes that the children have developed, if these are to be served as part of the celebratory performance

Previous learning

Discuss all the previous sessions and the written work that children have developed as a result of those sessions.

CONSIDER

Health & Safety

Assess and evaluate hazards and risks in your setting. See the health and safety chapter.

LESSON OBJECTIVES

We are planning a celebratory performance of many different types of writing developed through a sense of place.

National Curriculum Content

- Listen to and discuss a wide range of poetry.
- Prepare poems to read aloud and to perform, showing understanding through intonation, tone, volume and action.
- Retrieve and record information from non-fiction books and articles.

ADULT ROLES

- Support the children in selecting poems, recipe books and guides they have written that can be used in a celebratory performance.

WARM UP IDEAS

Discuss the warm up activities children have done that have all been linked to the five different senses. Groups plan and lead a warm up game linked to one of the senses, either one of those they have experienced or their own idea.

Introductory activity (individual)

Discuss what they have learned about the outdoor space and how they have used the five senses to explore it. Encourage them to select five different natural items that they can write on. They will need to think about each of the five senses and develop a word or a sentence linked to each one, e.g. choose some bark, a leaf, a stick or a flat stone. For example, for the sense of sight, they could write 'beautiful coloured leaves' on a natural item. For the sense of sound, they could write 'the sound of woodpeckers'.

Once they have completed this task, all the natural objects can be placed on the branch. The children can then decorate the branch with craft items to create a sensory memory sculpture.

MAIN ACTIVITIES

Our sensory place

Challenge 1 (groups of four)

Sensory gardens

Talk to the children about the outdoor place and how they have explored it through their senses. They will need to draw upon these experiences in this challenge, as they develop a sensory garden that includes all five senses.

Refer to the sensory garden resources for schools and ask groups to discuss and consider the following:

- How big is the garden going to be?
- Look at a list of sensory plants and decide which plants could be planted here to include all the five senses.
- Can any edible plants be planted? What will they taste like?
- What will the plants look like? Will they be colourful?
- Will the plants attract wildlife?
- What will the plants be like to touch?
- Could the garden be part of a sensory trail?

For further information, see the preparation section.

Encourage each group to develop a guide to the sensory garden they have planned. This could be an interactive guide with an oral and written element.

Challenge 2 (groups of four)

Plan and prepare a celebratory performance

Talk to the children about the work they have created as a result of the sense of place unit and explain that they are going to plan a celebratory performance and presentation of their work. They will need to include interactive guides, poetry they have developed, musical instruments, recipes, stories, etc. They could present their work on a journey through the outdoor place. An invited audience could travel with them through the outdoor place, using the interactive guide they have developed. They could stop at relevant points in the outdoor place and listen to stories and poems that the children have created. This could culminate in a whole-class performance beside the sensory memory sculpture. The children could then serve some of the autumnal delights they have cooked from their favourite forage recipes. The performance will need to be arranged for a later date to allow time to plan their performance.

PLENARY

Discuss with the children all five senses they have experienced in the outdoor area. How has the outdoor space changed during the sessions? What has been developed? Which is their favourite place to go? Where do they go to reflect? What senses have they developed through exploring the outdoor place? How has this impacted on their writing? Have they been inspired to write about this outdoor place?

Back in the classroom

- Develop a class book of sensory poems.
- Build on the interactive guide to the outdoor learning area so that it includes all five senses developed through the sessions.
- Have an open day for another class or parents to celebrate the work the children have developed through a sense of place.

EVALUATION/FOLLOW ON

- What went well today?
- Which children understood the concepts?
- Which children needed more help?
- Are there other resources you can use?
- Can you use some of the work developed to make an interactive display about a sense of place in the classroom?

Maths

In this unit, children will be using and applying maths in the real context of building fires and shelters, using tools and creating natural art. They will describe shapes, using the descriptive vocabulary associated with shape properties, positional language and direction, and use the vocabulary linked to calculation and estimation and measures, clearly linked to the 2014 Year 3 mathematics objectives, specifically geometry. The objectives are introduced and reinforced using team-building activities, including an introduction to 'Raccoon Circle' techniques, which provide opportunities to practise communication, social skills and teamwork. You can find over 150 Raccoon Circle activities in *The Revised and Expanded Book of Raccoon Circles* by Jim Cain and Tom Smith, and you can download a free collection of Raccoon Circle activities at: www.teamworkandteamplay.com. These activities promote the National Curriculum speaking and listening aims and provide opportunities for problem-solving and collaborative learning in the context of using and applying maths. They also provide 'assessment for learning' opportunities.

To support inclusive practice or to extend learning, the space, task, equipment and people (STEP) approach can be adopted throughout this unit. By changing the space, task, equipment or people, the activity can be made more challenging or easier to understand, enabling all pupils to take part in the activity, as explained in the assessment chapter in this book. To support differentiation and individual needs, the Year 2 objectives are also referenced where appropriate.

The main activities offer opportunities for adult-directed whole-group and smaller-group work, as well as opportunities for individual exploration and experimentation where appropriate. Timings will vary according to your setting, pupil experience and the support available. The children will be expected to work together in small groups with support from adults, as described in each progression.

You may wish to record the activities using a camera.

Natural connections

- Knowledge about trees
- Properties of wood
- Uses of and care for the environment.

Health and wellbeing

- Physical activity
- Teamwork
- Self-regulation and independence
- Risk-management
- Resilience and perseverance.

Word bank

Geometry – properties of shape

- horizontal
- vertical
- perpendicular and parallel lines
- 2D shapes
- 3D shapes

Geometry – position and direction

- greater/less than 90 degrees
- same orientation
- different orientation

Summary overview

Progression	Curriculum content	Learning experiences/activities
Lesson 1	Draw and make 2D shapes using modelling materials. Identify horizontal and vertical lines and pairs of perpendicular and parallel lines. Measure and compare lengths.	Children are introduced to team-building activities with a length of tubular webbing. This is used to 'shape up' a circle. They then 'shape up' a rectangle. They 'step in' to describe and state properties of these shapes. In groups, they make their own 2D shapes as modelled, and use these to explore and state the properties of the shapes they have made.
Lesson 2	Draw 2D shapes and make 3D shapes using modelling materials. Recognise 3D shapes in different orientations and describe them. Identify horizontal and vertical lines and pairs of perpendicular and parallel lines.	Children explore and use their knowledge of 2D and 3D shapes to investigate whether the shape of a fire base impacts on the effectiveness of a fire. In small groups they light a fire as modelled, understanding and managing the risks involved.
Lesson 3	Draw and make 2D shapes using modelling materials and describe them. Identify horizontal and vertical lines and pairs of perpendicular and parallel lines. Compare lengths and measure the perimeter of simple 2D shapes.	Children explore the properties of 2D shapes with an activity introducing and reinforcing key shape vocabulary. They are introduced to square lashing and use this to create a rectangular frame, satisfying shape properties criteria. They may also create a frame shape of their choice.
Lesson 4	Draw 2D shapes and make 3D shapes using modelling materials. Recognise 3D shapes in different orientations and describe them. Identify horizontal and vertical lines and pairs of perpendicular and parallel lines.	Children use team-building activities with a length of tubular webbing to explore the properties of different triangles, linking to structure strength in Progression 5. They are introduced to 'random pairing' and 'walk and talk' communication and idea-sharing activities.
Lesson 5	Draw 2D shapes and make 3D shapes using modelling materials. Recognise 3D shapes in different orientations and describe them. Identify horizontal and vertical lines and pairs of perpendicular and parallel lines.	Children revise and use their knowledge of the strength and properties of triangles in an introductory problem-solving activity, before building a strong temporary shelter frame using sticks. They describe the properties of their shelter using shape vocabulary. There is the option to use tools.
Lesson 6	Make 2D shapes using modelling materials and describe them. Identify horizontal and vertical lines and pairs of perpendicular and parallel lines. Compare lengths of simple 2D shapes.	Children are introduced to stick weaving. They make 2D shapes, satisfying shape property criteria, and describe these using mathematical vocabulary. There is the opportunity to use tools.

PREPARATION

In preparation for progression 2, identify the area to be used as a fire-lighting area, such as a cleared area.

Become familiar with the water knot used to join the lengths of tubular webbing. This knot, also known as a tape knot, is strong under pressure but also easy to undo after use. See www.bloomsbury.com/NC-Outdoors for instructions.

Resources

- One 13 m length of tubular webbing or soft rope (readily available online)

- Four 6 m lengths of tubular webbing or soft rope (or more if needed, e.g. in the case of larger classes) for group work

This progression introduces Raccoon Circles. You can find over 150 Raccoon Circle activities in *The Revised and Expanded Book of Raccoon Circles* by Jim Cain and Tom Smith.

CONSIDER

Health & Safety

Assess and evaluate hazards and risks in your setting. See the health and safety chapter.

LESSON OBJECTIVES

We are exploring and identifying the properties of 2D shapes.

National Curriculum Content

- Draw and make 2D shapes using modelling materials.

- Identify horizontal lines and pairs of perpendicular and parallel lines.

- Measure and compare lengths.

- Year 2: Some children may identify, describe and compare the properties of 2D and 3D shapes.

ADULT ROLES

- Support with making the shapes only where necessary, e.g. to control safety or to promote 'on task' behaviour, as a key element of the tasks is to work as a team.

- Allow experimentation but consider safety.

- Ask questions, encouraging the use of mathematical vocabulary.

WARM UP IDEAS

Explain that over the next six weeks, the children will be exploring maths in the outdoors. Ask the children what maths they have done outdoors in the past. Tell them that today's lesson will be exploring properties of shape.

Next week they will be lighting fires, but this week they will explore suitable spaces for a fire.

Which shape would work best for a group so that the heat is fairly shared and safely accessible from any direction?

- Why do we need to create a safety zone around a fire?

- What shape would be best for this?

- Would it matter if it were a different shape?

- What other shapes could the safety zone be?

- What would be the things to consider, such as equal access to the fire?

Properties of 2D shapes

Join the ends of the 13 m webbing using a water knot. Explain that children are going to create different 2D shapes using the tubular webbing.

Challenge 1 (whole class)

Team building

Children hold the webbing 'overhand' (over the top of the tape, rather than grabbing it from below) and stand in a circle.

1. Note who is nearest the knot – name them the 'Keeper of the knot'.
2. Working together, they pass the knot around the circle in an anticlockwise direction to acclimatise themselves to the feel and effect. Ensure that the overhand rule is kept.
3. As it returns to the Keeper, everyone raises the tape above their heads and then back to waist height again. Add a cheer!
4. Repeat but in a clockwise direction, ensuring that the overhand rule is kept.
5. How quickly do they think they could pass the knot? Count as the knot is passed.
6. Could they pass it faster?
7. Are the children quicker passing the knot clockwise or anticlockwise? Try out both options to see.

Challenge 2 (whole class)

Shape up - make and describe the properties of a circle

1. Holding the tape at waist height, the class works together to 'shape up' or make a perfect circle.
2. To check that it is a perfect circle, carefully work together to place it on the ground. This may take a few attempts. Just try again, remedying any problems as they occur.
3. When it is on the ground, the class walk around the outside of the circle, looking to see whether it matches the properties of a circle, in order to get a different perspective. The message is that sometimes it is important to view things from someone else's perspective.

4. When they are back in their start positions again, demonstrate how one person at a time can step over the tape and into the circle to give information. This is called 'step in'.
5. Ask: 'What are the properties of a circle?'
6. Children 'step in' to state one property of a circle, such as:
   - It has no corners or edges.
   - It is a two-dimensional curved shape.
   - It has infinite lines of symmetry.
   - It has a diameter.

Some children may be able to use 'radius' and 'circumference'.

Challenge 3 (class divided into four)

Make and describe the properties of a rectangle

Using the smaller lengths of tubular webbing, in groups, repeat steps 1 to 6 above, working this time to make a perfect rectangle.

1. Identify and describe the properties of the shape.
2. 'Step in' to the rectangle to state one of the properties.
3. How can you make sure that the opposite sides are the same length? Try out any ideas.
4. What measures can you use, e.g. paces, hands, feet, number of people?
5. How can we make sure that it is symmetrical?
6. Can they identify the lines of symmetry? Ask one or more of the children to walk along a line of symmetry. Name this action 'Walk the line'.

Challenge 4 (class divided into four)

Make and describe 2D shapes

Repeat steps 1 to 6 above but make a shape of their own as a group, using the shorter lengths of tubular webbing. Use 'step in' and 'walk the line'.

Encourage the children to state what they have found out about shape properties. Ask the children which shape might be best for keeping everyone warm around a fire, or for enabling everyone to see each other easily?

- What went well and why?
- What didn't go as well as expected?
- What could be changed?
- Who stood out and why?

PREPARATION

Identify the area to be used as a fire-lighting area. Surround this with well-defined markers such as large branches or tree stump seats to create the safety zone.

Sticks for fuel may need to be pre-collected and dried, then redistributed in the learning area for the children to find.

See additional information in the health and safety chapter.

Resources

- Additional adult support for fire-lighting
- Fire steels or fire striker
- Kindling such as cotton make-up pads opened up and wiped with petroleum jelly or hay or straw rolled into balls or twisted together
- Collection of fuel such as dry sticks of varying lengths and widths
- Water to extinguish the fires
- Heat-resistant gloves

CONSIDER

Health & Safety

Assess and evaluate hazards and risks in your setting. See the health and safety chapter.

LESSON OBJECTIVES

We are using our knowledge of 2D and 3D shapes to light a fire and to understand (and manage) the risks involved.

National Curriculum Content

- Draw 2D shapes and make 3D shapes using modelling materials.
- Recognise 3D shapes in different orientations and describe them.
- Identify horizontal and vertical lines and pairs of perpendicular and parallel lines.
- Year 2: Some children may identify, describe and compare the properties of 2D and 3D shapes.

ADULT ROLES

- Control safety and promote 'on task' behaviours.
- Encourage independence, working with a partner or as a team for support.
- Model the activity, acknowledging the tricky parts, recognising the difficulty and being positive about the management of the difficulty.
- Allow experimentation but consider safety.
- Ask questions, encouraging the use of mathematical vocabulary.

WARM UP IDEAS

Explain that today's lesson will be using fire-building to explore the properties of shape. Revise Progression 1. Which shape did they decide was a suitable one to surround a fire?

Which would work best for a group so that the heat is fairly shared and safely accessible from any direction?

Name properties of a circle that satisfy these criteria, e.g. all points on the circle are the same distance (equidistant) from the centre point or that the radius is the distance from the centre to any point on the edge of the circle. This can be demonstrated by repeating the 'shape up' activity from Progression 1, but allow additional time for this.

Discuss: Why do we need to create a safety zone around a fire? Revise key safety points.

MAIN ACTIVITIES

Fire-building

Explain that the children are going to explore 3D shapes whilst making their own small fires.

Discuss the positives and negatives of fire and key safety points outlined in the health and safety chapter.

Can the children remember the fire triangle theory from prior learning? Or explain that fires need heat, fuel and oxygen?

Challenge 1 (whole class)

Collect sticks (fuel) for the fire

1. Explain that the next activity will take ten minutes. Draw a circle on the ground to represent a clock face. Use two sticks to represent the minute and hour hands.
2. Ask: 'The time is... now. What will the time be in ten minutes?'
3. Ask the children to collect snappy sticks no wider than the width of one finger and no longer than a hand – they can of course be snapped to this length. The 'snap' shows that they are dry and able to burn.
4. The children collect their sticks then gather at the prepared fire-pit area.
5. The children sort their sticks, as when the fire is lit, the thinnest and smallest sticks will be used as fuel first, before gradually adding the broader ones.

Challenge 2 (whole class)

How to light a fire safely using 3D shapes

Introduce and model key step-by-step fire-lighting principles, reinforcing safety and shape vocabulary.

1. Place a container of water near the fire circle.
2. Make a clear space.
3. Create a square base. Does it have to be square? What are the properties of a square?
4. Build a 3D pyramid by pressing one end of the sticks into the ground, then tapering them towards one another at the other end. Does it have to be a pyramid? What are the properties of a pyramid and why might these help with the fire-lighting process, for example by acting as a chimney?

5. Add the fuel (thinnest sticks, dry lichen, straw sphere or 'pulled' cotton make-up pads).
6. Add heat (using the fire striker).
7. Show how to maintain the fire by carefully adding the smaller twigs. Model the safe stance position with one knee on the ground.
8. Give the children fire strikers to practise making sparks, taking turns. Count five attempts before passing it to a partner to have a go. Adult tip: Check the acute angle of the striker.

Challenge 3 (groups of four to six)

Create a shaped fire base and see which one is most effective

Children explore which shaped base works best for fire-lighting – rectangle (including square) or triangle?

- Identify, compare and name the differences between the shapes.
- How can you ensure that it is symmetrical?
- Use positional vocabulary to describe to a partner where to place the sticks.
- As they create the fire pyramid, discuss the properties, e.g. how many sides does a triangular or square-based pyramid have?
- They light their fire with adult supervision once their bases have been prepared.

PLENARY

Encourage the children to explain what they have been doing in the session and state what they have found out about shapes.

Which shaped base is the most effective and why?

EVALUATION/FOLLOW ON

- What went well and why?
- What didn't go as well as expected?
- What could be changed?
- Who stood out and why?

PREPARATION

If necessary, source a collection of sticks suitable for making a frame beforehand. If the children are not going to use tools, cut them to size.

Practise square lashing and clove hitch techniques. Instructions can be found at www.bloomsbury.com/NC-Outdoors.

Resources

- Four 50 cm lengths of coloured lashing, string or cordage for each child, plus extras
- Optional: lengths of wired raffia can be used as an alternative to lashing
- Collection of sticks
- Bow saws
- Loppers
- Sheath knife or scissors
- Safety gloves

Previous learning

Recap the previous session and the 2D and 3D shapes that they have been using to make fires.

How many shapes can they name?

CONSIDER

Health & Safety

Assess and evaluate hazards and risks in your setting. See the health and safety chapter.

LESSON OBJECTIVES

We are exploring 2D shape properties to create a frame using square lashing.

National Curriculum Content

- Draw and make 2D shapes using modelling materials and describe them.
- Identify horizontal and vertical lines and pairs of perpendicular and parallel lines.
- Compare lengths and measure the perimeter of simple 2D shapes.
- Year 2: Some children may identify, describe and compare the properties of 2D and 3D shapes.

ADULT ROLES

- Encourage independence, working with a partner or as a team for support.
- Model the activity yourself, acknowledging the tricky parts and being positive about the management of any difficulties.
- Allow experimentation but consider safety.
- Ask questions, encouraging the use of mathematical vocabulary.

WARM UP IDEAS

Explain to the children that in Progression 5 they will be making shelters but that this week they will be learning how to join sticks together using square lashing, to give them skills that they will use to make their shelter structures sturdy.

If they have done this before in Key Stage 1 then it will be a revision session for joining techniques, but the main focus will be on how this can support and extend their maths learning.

Introductory activity (groups of four)

Groups collect 12 sticks as long as their forearm and 12 small sticks as long as their hands, then work together to make a design or picture that contains the most geometric shapes possible.

Use mathematical vocabulary to describe properties, e.g. number of sides, perpendicular and parallel lines, angles greater or less than 90 degrees, lines of symmetry, etc.

2D shapes and frame-making

Explain that the children will be exploring 2D shapes using sticks to make a frame, such as a picture frame or mirror frame. What else could it be? This may affect the sticks that the children choose.

The children each choose four sticks for their frames. The sticks will need to be wider than their thumbs and as long as their arm from elbow to fingertips.

If the children are to use tools, they can cut them to size, following safety instructions detailed in the health and safety chapter.

Challenge 1 (in pairs)

Explore the properties of different 2D shapes using the sticks

- What shape would be best for a frame? Does it have to be a square?

- What would be the things to consider?

- What other shapes could the frame be? Make and try them.

- Explore and identify the differences in properties of the shapes, using the vocabulary from the introductory activity.

- Identify the lines of symmetry. How can you ensure that the frame is symmetrical?

- Does a line have to be vertical to be symmetrical? What difference would this make to the properties?

- How can you make sure that the sides are the same length?

What measures can you use, e.g. finger lengths, hand spans or widths? Some children may be able to estimate the perimeter of the shape.

Challenge 2 (in pairs)

Create a rectangular frame using square lashing

Introduce and model the square lashing technique by joining two sticks in a cross.

1. Tie a clove hitch to the upright stick, ensuring that the long (live) end of the cord is towards you.

2. Place the other stick across the upright stick.

3. Pass the live end of the cord down and over the cross stick then around the back of the upright stick.

4. Bring the cord to the front by travelling it under the cross stick.

5. Then bring the cord up and over the cross stick.

6. Repeat the instructions three to five times, making sure that the cord is pulled tightly to keep it neat.

7. Next, wind the cord three times between the two sticks and pull as tightly as you can.

8. Finally, tie the two live and dead ends of the cord together with a square knot.

The children use lashing to join sticks to make a frame shape of their choice.

They follow the instructions above to join the sticks using square lashing. A rectangular or triangular frame may be easiest.

What will they use their frame for? For example:

- Make a picture using found objects from the outdoor learning area and frame it.

- Take a portrait photograph of them in the frame.

- Make it a window or door frame.

- Add more cord to it and turn it into a mini cargo net climbing frame or weaving loom.

Evaluate the effectiveness of their frames and discuss pros and cons of their chosen shape.

How did they apply the properties of the shape to their designs?

- What went well and why?

- What didn't go as well as expected?

- What could be changed?

- Who stood out and why?

PREPARATION

Source the tubular webbing lengths.

Rehearse the water knot (or tape knot).

You can find over 150 Raccoon Circles activities in *The Revised and Expanded Book of Raccoon Circles* by Jim Cain and Tom Smith.

Resources

- One 13 m length of tubular webbing or soft rope
- Three 6 m lengths of tubular webbing or soft rope (or more if needed, e.g. in the case of larger classes)

Previous learning

Revise last week's creation of 2D shapes and knots.

CONSIDER

Health & Safety

Assess and evaluate hazards and risks in your setting. See the health and safety chapter.

LESSON OBJECTIVES

We are working as a team to explore and describe the properties of triangles.

National Curriculum Content

- Draw 2D shapes and make 3D shapes using modelling materials.
- Recognise 3D shapes in different orientations and describe them.
- Identify horizontal and vertical lines and pairs of perpendicular and parallel lines.
- Year 2: Some children may identify, describe and compare the properties of 2D and 3D shapes.

ADULT ROLES

- Encourage independence, working with a partner or as a team for support.
- Model the activity yourself, acknowledging the tricky parts and being positive about the management of the difficulty.
- Allow experimentation but consider safety.
- Ask questions, encouraging the use of mathematical vocabulary.

WARM UP IDEAS

Remind the children that in Progression 5 they will be creating shelter structures, but that this week, they will explore the properties of different triangles.

Why is this? Triangles are the strongest shape to use for structures, as the forces are spread evenly through the three sides.

Why wouldn't a rectangle be as strong? Adding diagonal bracing (making a triangle) can help.

Where have they seen triangles used to strengthen structures?

Are there any examples in the school setting, e.g. in climbing or swing frames? If so, have a look at them to see how they are used to strengthen and stabilise the structure.

MAIN ACTIVITIES

Triangle teams

Reintroduce the Raccoon Circle activities, using the long length of tubular webbing with ends joined with a water knot for the following activities:

Challenge 1 (whole class)

'Random pairing' and 'Walk and talk'

This is a great way to give children the chance to interact with children outside of their immediate friendship group. It is also a way of assessing learning by listening to the conversations!

1. Holding the webbing at waist height, the class works together to make a circle.
2. Carefully work together to place it on the ground. This may take a few attempts. Just try again, remedying any problems as they occur.
3. Every other child steps into the circle so that an equal number of children are outside and inside the circle.
4. 'Insiders' turn to the right and 'outsiders' turn to the left.
5. On your signal, the insiders and outsiders walk around the circle in opposite directions, e.g. the insiders anticlockwise and the outsiders clockwise.
6. Once the children have walked around the circle and a bit more, call out 'Stop!' and the children turn to face the person nearest to them – an outsider facing an insider.
7. This is now their talking and sharing partner to share ideas and talk through answers.
8. The children stand shoulder to shoulder in their relative positions (with tubular webbing between them on the ground) and all walk in the same direction, e.g. clockwise.
9. As they walk, they talk – but not at the same time!
10. The insider is the listener; the outsider is the talker.
11. Ask the children to share what they have learned so far about the properties of shapes. What was the best activity and what did they learn from it? What new words can they remember and use?
12. The children swap places and roles at the knot.

Challenge 2 (whole class)

Shape up - make and describe the properties of an equilateral triangle

Use raccoon circles to shape up and explore the properties of triangles.

1. Holding the tape at waist height, the whole group works together to make a perfect equilateral triangle.
2. To check that it is a perfect triangle, carefully work together to place it on the ground. This may take a few attempts. Just try again, remedying any problems as they occur.
3. When it is on the ground, as a class walk around the outside of the triangle, looking to see whether it matches the properties of a triangle, in order to get a different perspective.
4. How can they measure the sides? What could they use to check?
5. When they are back in their start positions again, ask volunteer children to 'step in' one at a time to state one property of the triangle, such as 'it has three sides of equal length' or 'all angles are equal'.

Challenge 3 (in groups of four)

Make different triangles and describe their properties

Groups work together to make a specific triangle, e.g. make an equilateral triangle, make a right-angled triangle, make a triangle of their choice, following the instructions modelled above.

PLENARY

Share their triangles with the whole class, identifying the properties of the triangles and discussing the elements of teamwork used to complete the task.

Using the 'Walk and talk' activity above, the children explain to their walk and talk partner what they have found out about shapes and about working together.

EVALUATION/FOLLOW ON

- What went well and why?
- What didn't go as well as expected?
- What could be changed?
- Who stood out and why?

PREPARATION

If necessary, source a collection of suitable sticks prior to the session.

If the children are not going to use tools, cut the sticks to size.

Practise the square lashing technique prior to the session.

Instructions can be found at www.bloomsbury.com/NC-Outdoors.

Resources

- Sufficient sticks to make shelter structures (e.g. garden withies)
- Longer lightweight poles (e.g. bamboo or coppiced branches)
- Lengths of thin lashing or thick string
- Tarpaulins (optional)
- Loppers
- Safety gloves

Previous learning

The children may have previously made shelters outside school.

Revise last week's exploration of triangles.

CONSIDER

Health & Safety

Assess and evaluate hazards and risks in your setting. See the health and safety chapter.

LESSON OBJECTIVES

We are learning to identify and use 2D and 3D shapes in shelter frames.

National Curriculum Content

- Draw 2D shapes and make 3D shapes using modelling materials.
- Recognise 3D shapes in different orientations and describe them.
- Identify horizontal and vertical lines and pairs of perpendicular and parallel lines.
- Year 2: Some children may identify, describe and compare the properties of 2D and 3D shapes.

ADULT ROLES

- Encourage independence, working with a partner or as a team for support.
- Model the activity yourself, acknowledging the tricky parts and being positive about the management of any difficulties.
- Allow experimentation but consider safety.
- Ask questions, encouraging the use of mathematical vocabulary.
- Ensure that the structures are stable before the children enter.

WARM UP IDEAS

Tell the children that they will be exploring 2D and 3D shapes by creating shelter structures and using their knowledge of triangles to make structures stable and strong.

Introductory activity

Collect sticks from the area and make different triangles. Which ones can they name and describe?

Can the children state why triangles are the strongest shape to use for structures, i.e. the forces are spread evenly through the three sides?

What examples of triangles in structures can they remember from design and technology, e.g. adding diagonal bracing on a climbing or swing frame?

MAIN ACTIVITIES

2D shapes and 3D shelters

What experience do the children have of shelter- and den-building? Emphasise that the focus today is to consider which 3D shapes make the most effective dens. What would 'effective' mean in this case?

Challenge 1 (in pairs or groups of four)

Use their knowledge of 3D shape to create a temporary shelter

Children create a framework big enough for the whole group to fit into.

As they work together to complete the task, ask them:

- To describe the rough shape of the structure, e.g. prism, cone, cube, etc.

- What shape names and properties do the 'faces' of the shelter-frame have?

- What horizontal/perpendicular/ parallel lines are there in your structure?

- Are there any triangles in the structure? If so, can the children name the types of triangles?

- What angles can you find in your structure? Which ones are more than or less than a right angle?

- Is there a link between the variety of angles and the strength of the shelter? How do you know? Could this be tested in some way?

- Does every structure have the same number or type of angles? If not, why not?

- Is there an optimum number of triangles or angles and a link to the effectiveness of the shelter?

Optional: Tool use to cut sticks to size or remove unwanted spurs.

Add additional detail to the shelters, such as tarpaulins or a few home comforts, and allow time to explore their structures fully.

Allow the children to have a period of quiet reflection within the structures.

If possible, allow the structures to remain in place for the next session.

PLENARY

Evaluate the effectiveness of the shelters and discuss pros and cons of each one, giving reasons.

Does the shape of the shelter or the 2D shapes used in the sides (faces) make a difference? And if so, in what way?

EVALUATION/FOLLOW ON

- What went well and why?

- What didn't go as well as expected?

- What could be changed?

- Who stood out and why?

PREPARATION

If necessary, source suitable flexible twigs, such as willow sticks. If the twigs are dry, soak them for a couple of days before the lesson.

If the children are not going to use tools, cut the twigs to size.

Master the twisting and weaving techniques prior to the session.

Resources

- 1 m lengths of soft pliable twigs (such as willow)
- Secateurs
- Loppers
- Safety gloves

Previous learning

Which wood makes a good fire? Which is strongest?

Do they recognise different trees in the outdoor area? What sort of wood makes a good shelter?

CONSIDER

Health & Safety

Assess and evaluate hazards and risks in your setting. See the health and safety chapter.

LESSON OBJECTIVES

We are learning to use wood-weaving to create 2D shapes.

National Curriculum Content

- Make 2D shapes using modelling materials.
- Identify horizontal and vertical lines and pairs of perpendicular and parallel lines.
- Compare lengths of simple 2D shapes.
- Year 2: Some children may identify, describe and compare the properties of 2D and 3D shapes.

ADULT ROLES

- Encourage independence, working with a partner or as a team for support.
- Model the activity yourself, acknowledging the tricky parts and being positive about the management of the difficulty.
- Allow experimentation but consider safety.
- Ask questions, encouraging the use of mathematical vocabulary.

WARM UP IDEAS

Review the structures from the previous week. Are they still standing?

What shapes made the structures strong?

What other elements made the structures successful, e.g. working together as a team to communicate and share ideas?

Discuss what it was like being inside the shelters. How did it make them feel? Did it feel special in any way?

Introduce this week's challenge of creating 2D shaped decorations for their area (to make the area more special), using natural materials and their knowledge of shape.

2D shape wood-weaving

Challenge 1 (whole class)

How to bend a stick to make a 2D shape

Before introducing the weaving technique, model and explore how to create simple 2D shapes by bending one long piece of the softwood, e.g. twice to make a triangle, three times to make a square, etc., ensuring that the edge lengths match the properties criteria, such as parallel opposite sides in the square or rectangle.

Challenge 2 (whole class)

How to make a woven right-angled triangle

1. Hold the willow stick by the thick end (shaft).
2. Make a bend in the willow shaft about one third of the way up from the bottom.
3. Explain that where the bends are made determines the side length.
4. Next make another bend about 5 cm further up, and use the bends to shape the willow stick into what looks like a number four (like this - 4).
5. Show how the extra length (formed after making the crossed part of the '4') can be woven to fill the inside of the triangle outline by twisting it back over the 'shaft' and weaving it under and around the outer side of the triangle by weaving over and under two of the sides of the triangle, as shown.
6. Keep weaving the willow over and under the two sides of the triangle, gradually filling the shape from the bottom to the top with woven willow.
7. Model how to safely use secateurs or loppers to cut willow or softwood to length.

Challenge 3 (individual or in pairs)

Create a woven shape

Children work individually or with a partner to follow the model to create different 2D shapes using softwood or willow.

- What properties do they need to consider? State these.
- Can they identify any lines of symmetry?
- If so, how can we make sure that it is symmetrical, e.g. by approximating or measuring where the bend will be made to create side length?
- Are there any parallel lines? How do you know?
- Some children may be able to name the angles in their shape.

Some children may wish to use the secateurs to cut lengths of willow.

Encourage them to estimate or roughly measure the lengths of the different shapes made in the class.

Evaluate the effectiveness of their woven shapes and discuss. How did they apply the properties of the shape to their designs?

- What went well and why?
- What didn't go as well as expected?
- What could be changed?
- Who stood out and why?

Science

In this unit, children will be focusing on scientific skills and observation. Based on the Key Stage 2 science objectives identified in the 2014 National Curriculum for England, the children will be introduced to rocks, soils and fossils. They will be given the opportunity to develop their observations skills, pose their own questions and carry out simple scientific enquiries to answer them. They will make fires, build volcanoes and develop their own fossils in a quest to find out more about rocks and the rock cycle.

To support inclusive practice or to extend learning, the space, task, equipment and people (STEP) approach can be adopted throughout this unit. By changing the space, task, equipment or people, the activity can be made more challenging or easier to understand, enabling all pupils to take part in the activity, as explained in the assessment chapter in this book.

The children will be expected to work as a whole class directed by the teacher, together in small groups with support from adults, and independently. The role of the adult is to lead the sessions safely, modelling the activities, allowing experimentation and independence whilst providing direct support and resilience.

You may wish to record the activities using a camera.

Natural connections

- Enhanced awareness of local natural environments and changes within them
- Using observation skills, looking at patterns created by natural materials.

Health and wellbeing

- Physical activity
- Being focused and attentive
- Team-building
- Emotional resilience
- Independence.

Word bank

Rocks

- rocks
- fossils
- soils
- grains
- crystals
- erosion
- rock cycle

Scientific

- grouping
- sorting
- classifying
- observations
- fair test
- predictions

Summary overview

Progression	Curriculum content	Learning experiences/activities
Lesson 1	Compare and group together different kinds of rocks on the basis of their appearance and simple physical properties.	The children will be given the opportunity to observe and classify rocks according to their properties. They will make and learn how to tie different knots and use these skills to make simple tools from rocks and string. They will make a fire and look at the tools used to make a fire.
Lesson 2	Compare and group together different kinds of rocks on the basis of their appearance and simple physical properties. Identify differences, similarities or changes related to simple scientific ideas and processes.	The children will have the opportunity to create their own designs using the work of Andy Goldsworthy to inspire their work. They will build sculptures from rocks and they will be given the opportunity to test how strong their structures are by carrying out their own fair test.
Lesson 3	Recognise that soils are made from rock and organic matter. Ask relevant questions and use different types of scientific enquiries to answer them.	Children will hear the story of Roger the Rock who becomes Simon Soil. They will look at the process of the rock cycle and build their own sculptures to retell the story of how Roger the Rock becomes Simon Soil. Children will also carry out a simple test with rocks and paint to observe erosion.
Lesson 4	Recognise that soils are made from rock and organic matter. Use straightforward scientific evidence to answer questions or to support their findings	The children will make observations of soil. They will go on a bug hunt to find out what lives in soil. They will have the opportunity to make a wormery and will be encouraged to record their observations and findings in relation to the wormery.
Lesson 5	Geography: Describe and understand key aspects of volcanoes. Report on findings from enquiries, including oral and written explanations, displays or presentations of results and conclusions.	Children will have the opportunity to make a volcano out of soil and sand. They will look at the key features of volcanoes and label them. They will look at volcanic rock and develop their understanding of how volcanic rock is formed.
Lesson 6	Describe in simple terms how fossils are formed when things that have lived are trapped within rock.	Children will have the opportunity to make their own fossil in this session. They will discover how fossils are made and what can be contained within rocks. They will talk about dinosaurs and the significance of fossils in their discovery. They will make their own dinosaurs.

PREPARATION

Ensure that there is a selection of rocks in the outdoor learning area. Bring in some different rocks for the children to look at, e.g. slate, granite, marble and volcanic rock, which the children may not be able to find on the site.

Resources

- Selection of rocks, including slate and granite
- Magnifying glasses and hand lenses
- Plastic hoops for classifying rocks
- String
- Selection of tools, including mallets and hammers, and pictures of more primitive tools
- For help with knots, see www.bloomsbury.com/NC-Outdoors
- *Go Wild!* by Jo Schofield and Fiona Danks (optional)
- Optional: fire-lighting kit including flint and steel, storm kettle, water to extinguish the fire and hot chocolate ingredients

Previous learning

Discuss with the children the meaning of the word 'properties' and what they know about materials and their properties.

CONSIDER

Health & Safety

Assess and evaluate hazards and risks in your setting. See the health and safety chapter.

LESSON OBJECTIVES

We are learning to compare different kinds of rocks on the basis of their simple physical properties.

National Curriculum Content

- Compare and group together different kinds of rocks on the basis of their appearance and simple physical properties.

ADULT ROLES

- Support the children in finding and describing a range of rocks made from different materials.
- Promote questioning and encourage the children to describe the rocks and their properties.

WARM UP IDEAS

Play the game 'Rock, paper, scissors'. In pairs, children place their hands behind their backs. On the count of three, they make a shape with their hands in front of their body of either a rock (clenched fist), paper (flat hand) or scissors (a cutting action with fingers). The winner is the object produced that overrides the other object. Scissors can cut paper, so scissors win. Paper will cover rock, so paper wins. Rock blunts scissors, so rock wins. If two objects are the same, you play again. Play three rounds and the winner is the best of three rounds.

Introductory activity

Explain that in this unit of work children will be exploring rocks. They will be observing the different properties of rocks and the different ways in which they can be used, e.g. for tool-making, etc. In pairs, they are going on a rock hunt. They will need to find rocks that are hard, soft or flaky, sharp and smooth. Once they have collected a range of rocks, encourage the children to pose their own questions about the rocks.

- What is the rock made from?
- What properties does the rock have?
- How many questions can they generate?

MAIN ACTIVITIES

Classifying rocks

Ask the children to work in pairs to continue their investigations. Give the children hand lenses and magnifying glasses so that they can observe the rocks more closely. Encourage the children to classify them according to their properties by placing them in a different hoop, e.g. a hoop for smoother rocks.

Challenge 1 (individual)
Tying knots

Ask the children to find two sticks. Give each child a piece of string. First encourage them to tie a reef knot. Place the right-hand string over the left-hand string and then left over right and tie. Then challenge them to make a clove hitch. Once they have managed to tie a clove hitch, challenge the children to fasten the two sticks together using a square lashing technique. Further advice on how to tie knots can be found at www.bloomsbury.com/NC-Outdoors.

Let the children practise these knots to secure two or more sticks together. They will use these knots in the next challenge.

Challenge 2 (in pairs)
Tool making

Show the children a range of tools made from different materials. Also share pictures of more primitive tools with the children. More information on making tools can be found in *Go Wild!* by Jo Schofield and Fiona Danks. Ask the children to look at the rocks they collected and to think about appropriate rocks for making tools using sticks and string. Discuss possible designs and how they might make them, e.g. hammer, cutting tool, axe, etc. Work in pairs to make a simple tool using sticks, stones and string. Will they need to use any tools to make their tool? Refer to the safe use of tools in the health and safety chapter.

Once the children have made their tools, ask them to consider:

- What purpose did they intend for their tool, e.g. cutting or hammering?
- How effective is their tool?
- What rock have they used? Why?
- Would they change anything about their tool to improve it?

Challenge 3 (whole class)
Extension activity – fire-lighting

Look at the flint and steel. What properties do these have? Discuss which part is flint and which is steel. Which is a rock and which is a metal?

Use a storm kettle to make hot chocolate.

Use the guidance in the health and safety chapter on safe fire-lighting to make a fire. Clear a space, make a base, build a pyramid, strike, light and feed. Talk about the importance of clearing all stones and rocks from where you are building the fire, as they may heat and explode. The reason they might explode is that if they have air or water trapped inside, it will expand and could shatter the rock when heated. Extinguish the fire safely after use.

PLENARY

Talk to the children about the tools they have made in the session. What do they now understand about the properties of rocks and stones? What do they understand about using materials for different purposes, e.g. cutting, hammering, etc.? Evaluate the final products.

Back in the classroom

Build a class collection of rocks with a range of different rock types. Encourage the children to identify the rocks and label the rocks and their properties. Encourage the children to pose questions about the rocks.

EVALUATION/FOLLOW ON

- What went well today?
- Which children understood the concepts?
- Which children needed more help?
- Are there other resources you can use?
- Can you use some of the materials collected to make a display of different materials in the classroom?

PREPARATION

Ensure that there is a selection of rocks in the outdoor learning area.

Bring in some different rocks for the children to work with, e.g. slate, granite, marble and different coloured rocks, which the children may not be able to find on the site.

Resources

- Images of artwork using stones and pebbles by Andy Goldsworthy

- A range of rocks, stones and pebbles

CONSIDER

Health & Safety

Assess and evaluate hazards and risks in your setting. See the health and safety chapter.

LESSON OBJECTIVES

We are learning to compare different kinds of rocks on the basis of their simple physical properties and to use them to make a sculpture.

National Curriculum Content

- Compare and group together different kinds of rocks on the basis of their appearance and simple physical properties.

- Identify differences, similarities or changes related to simple scientific ideas and processes.

- Art: Learn about great artists (Andy Goldsworthy).

ADULT ROLES

- Support the children in finding and describing a range of rocks and making images from different rocks.

- Promote questioning and encourage the children to describe the rocks and their properties.

WARM UP IDEAS

Children sit in a circle and play the game 'Zip, zap, bong'. This is a game to help them improve their concentration and listening skills. One child passes the 'zip' around the circle with two hands joined together palm to palm. Each child continues with this action as they pass the 'zip' around the circle. If they want to pass to someone across the circle, they use a 'zap' action. Their hands are still placed together and they point at the person across the circle and say 'zap'. If they want to change direction, they place both hands up in the air and say 'bong'. The child to the right of the person who said 'bong' then needs to continue with the zip action around the circle. Talk to the children about the importance of concentration.

Introductory activity

Talk to the children about the rock collection they are developing and remind them about the meaning of physical properties. Look at the different colours and textures of the rocks. Each child chooses a rock. Working in pairs, they describe the rock to their partner. What could it be used for? What it is made from? What are its properties? Swap roles.

MAIN ACTIVITIES

Comparing rocks

Talk to the children about the rock collection they are developing and remind them what 'physical properties' means. Look at the different colours and textures of the rocks. Each child chooses a rock. Working in pairs, they describe the rock to their partner. What could it be used for? What it is made from? What are its properties? The partners then swap roles.

Challenge 1 (in pairs)

Rock art

Show the children images of Andy Goldsworthy's work and discuss his use of natural objects to create art. Look at the designs and patterns that he created in his art. Ask the children to drop some stones on the ground and see whether it inspires a piece of art, abstract or otherwise. What can they see? In pairs, create their own artwork using rocks/stones, using Goldsworthy's designs to inspire them. They could use small rocks and stones of different colours, sizes and textures. Encourage the children to pose different questions about the rocks. What are the similarities and differences between the rocks they have used? What changes may have happened to the rocks to create their different shapes?

Challenge 2 (in pairs)

Tower of rocks

Ask the children to collect different stones and rocks that could be used to make a tower. Ask the children to consider the following:

- What properties will the rocks need to have?
- How can they use the stones to build a tower?
- How high can they make the tower?
- What structures can they create?
- What tests could they perform to test the strength of the towers?
- How would they ensure that it was a fair test?

Give the children time to look at the artwork and towers/sculptures they have created using different rocks and stones. What different stones have they used? Can they identify what any of the rocks or stones are made from? Which rocks are most effective in creating patterns and designs? Which rocks have they used to build a tower?

PLENARY

Discuss with the children the different ways they have used rocks within the session. How do the different rocks compare? What designs have they created? How have different rocks' properties supported their designs and ideas? Discuss how nature might inspire art.

Back in the classroom

Explore further the work of Andy Goldsworthy. Who is he? What other work has he created? Does he use other natural objects in his work? Can you create a classroom display inspired by his work?

EVALUATION/FOLLOW ON

- What went well today?
- Which children understood the concepts of the physical properties of rocks?
- Which children needed more help?
- Are there other resources you can use?
- Can you use some of the rocks collected to add to the collection in the classroom?
- Would a trip to a beach or quarry extend the children's learning?

PREPARATION

Ensure that you have a range of rocks available and a safe space to create the rock cycle through sculptures.

Resources

- Parachute
- Images of the rock cycle
- Play sand and a selection of rocks
- Ice cream tubs and paint

Previous learning

Ask the children what they know about rocks and their properties and what they have learned in previous sessions.

CONSIDER

Health & Safety

Assess and evaluate hazards and risks in your setting. See the health and safety chapter.

LESSON OBJECTIVES

We are learning to understand how rocks become soil/sand.

National Curriculum Content

- Recognise that soils are made from rock and organic matter.
- Ask relevant questions and use different types of scientific enquiries to answer them.

ADULT ROLES

- Support the children in finding and describing a range of rocks.
- Support them in creating sculptures to tell the story of Roger the Rock to Simon Soil.

WARM UP IDEAS

Whole class

Children stand in a circle holding a parachute. Give each child the name of a rock type, e.g. slate, marble, granite, etc. When the name of their rock is called, they run under the parachute. When 'rock' is called, they all raise the parachute and gather underneath to create a dome.

Introductory activity

Today the class will be investigating how rocks become soil. Check their understanding of the difference between the two.

Tell the children the a story about the rock cycle. You could create a story with characters in it, for example, 'Roger the Rock' and 'Simon the Soil'.

Discuss the different stages of the story with the children and encourage the children to break down the story into different parts to help them to remember it.

- Show the children images of the rock cycle.
- Encourage the children to look at a sample of soil.
- Look carefully to see what it is made from.
- Ask the children to pose their own questions as to how it has become soil.

The rock cycle

Challenge 1 (groups of four)

Retelling the rock cycle story

Ask children to retell the story to each other using a story train. The first person in the group starts the story and they then each have a turn within the group until the story is complete. Provide the children with some play sand and encourage them to find a selection of rocks. Once they have a collection, ask the children to create the stages of the story in small groups, as structures on the ground, in a storyboard. For example:

1. Start with a tall, rocky structure that starts to crack.
2. Cold action shows the rocks getting smaller.
3. Then bits chip off into a river, etc.
4. Children then retell the story of Roger the Rock through their mud and sand sculptures.
5. Can they take on the role of Roger the Rock and act out part of the story using their storyboards as a guide to retell the story of the rock cycle?

Challenge 2 (small groups)

Erosion extension activity

1. Using the rocks collected, dip a small selection of rocks in different coloured paints and place them on a piece of paper in an ice cream tub and put the lid on.
2. Shake the tub and then open it.
3. What patterns have been created with the paint?
4. What effect does it have on paper?
5. Do stones with different textures create different marks on the paper?
6. Explain that the rocks rubbing together are eroding and, over a long period of time, erosion causes rocks to crack and break.
7. What has happened to the rocks shaken in the ice cream tub? Have they started to break up? Have any cracks appeared in the rocks?

PLENARY

Talk to the children about the storyboards they created and look at the different rocks and sculptures they have used to recreate the story of the rock cycle. In pairs, ask the children to discuss what they have learned about the rock cycle and how rocks become soil. What do they understand about erosion and how rocks change over time?

Back in the classroom

- Can you develop a 3D image of the rock cycle back in the classroom?
- How can you recreate the parts of the cycle?
- Ask children to bring in any rocks to add to the class rock collection.
- Can they name the types of rocks they have collected?
- Can they bring in photos of any examples of erosion they have seen?

EVALUATION/FOLLOW ON

- What went well today?
- Which children understood the concepts?
- Which children needed more help?
- Are there other resources you can use?
- Can you use some of the rocks and soil collected to add to the rock and soil collection being developed in the classroom?

PREPARATION

Ensure that there is a safe place to work in where children can look for worms, etc.

Ensure that there is sufficient access to soil.

Resources

- Ropes
- Clear plastic tubs or bottles for a wormery https://schoolgardening.rhs.org.uk/Resources/Activity/Mini-wormery
- Dark card, ideally black
- Soil, sand, compost and small stones
- Worm food: grated carrot, vegetable peelings, dead leaves, etc.

Previous learning

Talk to the children about the previous session and what they now know about rocks and soils.

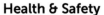

CONSIDER

Health & Safety

Assess and evaluate hazards and risks in your setting. See the health and safety chapter.

LESSON OBJECTIVES

We are investigating soil to find out what it is made from.

National Curriculum Content

- Recognise that soils are made from rock and organic matter.
- Use straightforward scientific evidence to answer questions or to support their findings.

ADULT ROLES

- Support the children in finding and describing soil.
- Promote questioning and encourage the children to describe the materials of the soil and what they have found.

WARM UP IDEAS

This game is like 'Simon says'. It develops concentration and listening skills. Using a rope, mark a line on the ground. Ask the children to stand in a line beside the rope. Tell them that they are now on an imaginary bank. If you call 'Simon Soil says "In the river!"', the children need to jump over the rope and into the river. If you just say 'In the river!' or 'Simon Soil says "On the bank!"', they shouldn't jump. If children move when the instructions are not called or jump in the wrong direction, then they are out. You could also include a zig-zag line for 'on the mountain' to add another instruction.

Introductory activity

Whole class

Look at a soil sample and discuss what it might be made from, based on what they have learned about the rock cycle. Does it contain anything else apart from broken-down rocks?

MAIN ACTIVITIES

Soil searching

Challenge 1 (in pairs)

Soil samples

Ask the children to collect a sample of soil in a container. Look at a soil sample and discuss between them what they can see it is made from. They may be able to see partially rotted leaves or minibeasts. Can they find a worm?

Tip: the school garden/cultivated earth may have more worms.

Challenge 2 (in groups of four or six)

Making a wormery

Ask two or three pairs to make groups and tell them that they are going to make a wormery.

Model the process of making a wormery and then allow them to make their own in their groups.

1. Cut the top off the bottle to make a lid or use a clear plastic container with a lid.
2. Fill the container with a layer of sand, then soil, then sand, then compost, etc. Make the layers damp with some water.
3. Place some worms in the container and watch them burrow down. Add the 'food', made of carrots, etc., to the top.
4. Wrap some black card around the bottle to make it dark. Worms do not like light, so if the bottle is uncovered they will burrow down the inside of the bottle so that they cannot be seen. The card can be removed for observations.
5. Ensure that the children wash their hands after handling worms and compost.

PLENARY

Look at the wormeries that the children have made. Encourage them to pose their own questions about the worms and the homes that they have made for them. What would they like to find out? For example, how quickly do the worms eat the food that is placed in the wormery? What happens to the layers of soil as the worms move around? What function might worms have in combining rocks and organic materials like leaves to make soil?

Back in the classroom:

Place the wormeries in a warm place in the classroom after this progression.

Allow time to observe what is happening during the following week. Encourage the children to make observations each day and record their findings. Can they find ways of presenting their findings in interesting and different ways to inform others of the results?

They should also keep their wormeries damp and ensure that the worms have enough food.

Leave it for a week and then discuss what they have seen happen. Does this answer any of their questions? Do they have new questions?

Note: Release the worms back to where they were found after one week.

EVALUATION/FOLLOW ON

- What went well today?
- Which children understood the concepts?
- Which children needed more help?
- Are there other resources you can use?

PREPARATION

Ensure that there is a safe space available for children to build their volcanoes.

Resources

- Images of volcanoes
- Cones
- Soil, rocks and stones
- Sand and test tubes
- Black card, magnifying glass and hand lenses
- Small cups and vinegar
- Lolly sticks, labels and small spades
- Bicarbonate of soda
- Food colouring: red, orange and yellow
- Soap pump and plastic tubes
- www.sciencekidsathome. com/science_experiments/ sand_1.html

Previous learning

Builds on previous progressions and children's knowledge about rocks and their properties.

CONSIDER

Health & Safety

Assess and evaluate hazards and risks in your setting. See the health and safety chapter.

LESSON OBJECTIVES

We are looking at sand and investigating what it is made from. We are learning about rocks and how volcanic rock is formed.

National Curriculum Content

- Report on findings from enquiries, including oral and written explanations, displays or presentations of results and conclusions.
- Geography: Describe and understand key aspects of volcanoes.

ADULT ROLES

- Support the children in making and labelling their volcano.
- Promote questioning and encourage the children to describe the materials and their properties that they have used to make their volcano.

WARM UP IDEAS

Ask the children to tell you what they know about valleys and volcanoes. What shapes are these features in the landscape? Place an even number of cones upside down and explain to the children that these are 'valleys'. Place the same number of cones with the point up and state that these are 'volcanoes'. Divide the class into two groups. Half of the children are 'valleys' and half are 'volcanoes'. On a signal, tell the children that they must turn the cones to the shape they have been given, i.e. children who are 'valleys' must turn as many cones as they can upside down. The winning team is the team with the most cones of their shape.

Introductory activity

Explain that today children will be investigating rocks and sand. They will need to pose questions and carry out enquiries to find out the answers to questions.

- Encourage the children to look at some soil.
- What do they know about soil?
- What is it made from?
- How do they know?
- What have they learned in previous sessions about soil?

MAIN ACTIVITIES

Volcano modelling

Challenge 1 (individual)

What is sand?

1. Ask the children to collect a pile of sand in their hand and take a careful look at what it is made of. What is each particle made up of – rock, glass, shells? Ask the children to sprinkle some sand onto black card and look at it through a magnifying glass or hand lens. Encourage the children to pose their own questions.

2. Give each child a test tube or small clear tube. Now tell the children that they are going to find out what happens when we add vinegar, which is an acid, to sand. Encourage the children to make their own predictions as to what might happen.

3. Ask the children to fill the test tubes with sand, leaving a small gap at the top of the tube for some vinegar. Add the vinegar and see what happens. If the sand bubbles, it has formed carbon dioxide, which is a gas. This indicates that there is calcium carbonate in the sand.

4. Ask the children what they think could be causing this in the sand. Where would you find calcium in the human body? Talk to children about the animals that they may find in the sand and what they could be made from. Shells or bones in the sand will contain calcium carbonate.

Challenge 2 (groups of four)

Making a volcano

Using their knowledge about the reactions of sand and vinegar, children will now make their own volcano. Discuss what the children know about volcanoes. Ask them to describe the key features of a volcano. Give each group some sand and soil and a selection of stones and small spades.

1. The children will need to build a large pyramid of sand.

2. The children will then need to place a reusable cup in the top of the pyramid of sand. This will be the crater.

3. The children will then place some bicarbonate of soda in the top of the sand crater.

4. They will then add some food colouring to the bicarbonate of soda.

5. Finally, they will add some vinegar and observe what happens.

Have a competition to see who can build the biggest volcano. Label key features using labels and lolly sticks. Create a space at the top of the volcano for the crater and place a cup in as the crater (you could also use a thin tube or a funnel). Encourage the children to predict what might happen when they add bicarbonate of soda, vinegar and food colouring. Ask the children to observe and record what happens. Can the children come up with a design to help it to explode using a pump action with a soap pump or plastic tube? Does using a funnel help? Why does it explode? Discuss the designs that the children have come up with to cause the volcano to explode. Take photos of the groups' volcanoes.

PLENARY

Talk to the children about what they have found out about sand and building a volcano. Discuss what sand is and what it started as originally. Talk to them about the rock cycle and what they know about the cycle from the previous session.

Back in the classroom

Build a 3D model of a volcano in the classroom and label the parts. Display with pictures of their volcanoes and the children's writing. What else would they like to know about volcanoes? Where do volcanoes occur? Why? Where in the world are there active volcanoes?

EVALUATION/FOLLOW ON

- What went well today?
- Which children understood the concepts?
- Which children needed more help?
- Are there other resources you can use?

PREPARATION

Review ideas in www.edenproject.com/learn/schools/lesson-plans/great-fossil-hunters.

Resources

- Fossils, or images of fossils
- Plaster of Paris
- Sand
- Air-drying clay
- Sticky tape
- Beach shells
- Paper and cocktail sticks
- Plastic gloves, spoons and yoghurt pots
- Stones, pebbles, rocks and pictures of dinosaurs

Previous learning

This progression builds on children's knowledge about the composition of sand and the formation of soil and rocks.

CONSIDER

Health & Safety

Assess and evaluate hazards and risks in your setting. See the health and safety chapter.

LESSON OBJECTIVES

We are learning to understand what a fossil is and how it is made and to replicate how fossils were discovered. We are looking at the properties of rocks and their ability to retain water.

National Curriculum Content

- Describe in simple terms how fossils are formed when things that have lived are trapped within rock.

ADULT ROLES

- Support the children in making their own fossils and understanding how fossils are made.
- Promote questioning and encourage the children to describe the properties of rocks with fossils.

WARM UP IDEAS

Let the children choose from the games they have played during this unit, e.g. 'Rock, paper, scissors', 'Valleys and volcanoes' or 'Simon Soil says'. Play one or two of these games and ask how it has linked to the work they have been doing about rocks, fossils and soils.

Introductory activity

Encourage the children to discuss what they know about fossils.

- Have they ever seen a fossil?
- Show the children some images or examples of fossils.
- What can they observe about rocks that contain fossils?
- How might a creature or plant have been captured as a fossil within rock?

MAIN ACTIVITIES

Fossils

Challenge 1 (individual)

Make your own fossil

Follow the instructions on how to make your own fossil using shells from the beach.

1. Give each child a loop of paper made into a circle and some air-drying clay.
2. Encourage the children to push the clay into the paper and mould it.
3. Select a shell and press it into the clay, keeping it still.
4. Remove the shell once a good imprint has been made.
5. Mix the plaster of Paris and pour it into the mould.
6. Remove the paper from the mould and make holes around the side of the mould using a cocktail stick.
7. Sprinkle some sand on top of the plaster of Paris.
8. Leave the clay to dry.
9. Follow the instructions on how to safely extract the fossil at the end of the day.

Record their observations and findings. What do they know about actual fossils forming? Explain how the hard shell would have been turned into rock to form a fossil, through minerals in water gradually solidifying it. What do they want to find out?

Challenge 2 (groups of four)

Dinosaur extension activity

Talk to the children about different sizes of fossils and dinosaurs. How are fossils linked to dinosaurs? How do we know that dinosaurs existed? Show the children pictures of dinosaurs. What can we know from fossils and what do we have to create theories about?

Challenge the small groups to create their own picture of a dinosaur using stones, rocks, pebbles and other natural materials. Once the dinosaurs have been completed, the groups visit dinosaurs created by other groups and ask questions.

PLENARY

Talk to the children about what they have found out about fossils. How have the fossils they have created worked? Which shells have created the best fossils? How might real fossils have been created? Which sort of rocks would we find them in? Do they want to find out more about fossils?

Back in the classroom

Plan a visit to the beach to further extend the children's knowledge of rocks, sand and fossils. Follow this up with some exciting writing on beach exploration, fossil hunting or a great dinosaur hunt.

EVALUATION/FOLLOW ON

- What went well today?
- Which children understood the concepts?
- Which children needed more help?
- Are there other resources you can use?
- Can you use some of the fossils made to add to the collection of rocks developing back in the classroom?

Geography

Based on the Key Stage 2 geography objectives identified in the 2014 National Curriculum for England, in this unit children build on geographical understanding and skills from Key Stage 1 to develop their locational knowledge and understanding of human and physical geography through the use of fieldwork. They are introduced to basic map skills: the principles of recognising their position on a map, following a trail and creating their own maps using keys within the school setting, working together to achieve teamwork challenges.

There are links to the British Orienteering resource 'Tri-O orienteering made easy (a complete introductory orienteering activity package for schools)', which is a free downloadable resource from www.britishorienteering.org.uk. British Orienteering is the national governing body for the sport of orienteering in the UK, which provides courses covering the basic skills of orienteering and access to competitions, both local and national.

To support inclusive practice or to extend learning, the space, task, equipment and people (STEP) approach can be adopted throughout this unit. By changing the space, task, equipment or people, the activity can be made more challenging or easier to understand, enabling all pupils to take part in the activity, as explained in the assessment chapter in this book.

The children will be expected to work as a whole class directed by the teacher, together in small groups or in pairs, either with support from adults or independently. The role of the adult is to lead the sessions safely, modelling the activities and encouraging the use of tactics and independence by giving the children time to come up with their own ideas, whilst providing positive support where appropriate.

You may wish to record the activities using a camera.

Natural connections

- Enhancing awareness of local environments (natural and built-up)
- Developing a sense of place
- Developing observational skills
- Understanding features of rivers.

Health and wellbeing

- Gaining confidence through acquiring and developing skills
- Physical activity
- Increasing focus and attention
- Selecting and applying skills
- Problem-solving and teamwork
- Considering questions of inclusion and developing trust, while describing and evaluating their own and others' performance.

Word bank

Maps

- physical and human geographical features
- aerial view
- symbols
- key

- control point
- control markers
- European countries and capital cities

Position, direction

- latitude
- longitude
- equator
- the Tropics of Cancer and Capricorn

- the Arctic and Antarctic Circles

Summary overview

Progression	Curriculum content	Learning experiences/activities
Lesson 1	Use fieldwork to observe human and physical features in the local area, using maps and plans.	Children explore and describe the area to a partner who has their eyes closed. They use simple shape orienteering to explore their position on the ground in relation to a map – 'Where am I?' They identify and mark a route on the map.
Lesson 2	Locate the world's countries, using maps. Name and locate counties and cities of the UK. Use maps, atlases, globes and digital mapping to locate countries. Use fieldwork to observe human and physical features in the local area.	The children follow an arrows trail (using sticks), finding control points and collecting jigsaw pieces to complete the puzzle, identifying countries. They may also draw a map based on the arrows trail and do a 'cross the river' problem-solving activity.
Lesson 3	Use maps to focus on Europe (countries and major cities). Use maps, atlases, globes and digital mapping to locate countries and major cities. Use fieldwork to observe human and physical features in the local area.	The children are introduced to map symbols using 'Kim's game'. They match symbols to physical features in the setting and follow an arrows trail (marked on a map), matching the names of European countries to their capital cities. They create their own arrows trail, drawing a map for it and identifying key features on the ground using symbols and a key.
Lesson 4	Use fieldwork to observe human and physical features in the local area.	Map symbol recognition is reinforced using a 'Kim's game' team relay. The children match symbols to physical features in the setting. They draw their own arrows trail on an unmarked map of the setting, matching more map symbols to key features and marking them on a map.
Lesson 5	Locate the world's countries, using maps to focus on Europe. Use fieldwork to observe human and physical features in the local area.	Using playground markings, the children take part in a 'follow the leader' and line balance warm up. They follow an arrows trail leading to letters marked on the playground to find letters forming the name of European countries. They may also use copies of the playground map to create their own arrows trail to give to another group.
Lesson 6	Locate the world's countries, using maps to focus on Europe. Use fieldwork to observe human and physical features in the local area.	The children explore inclusivity, leaving and joining groups in a hoop game: 'Over here!' They find specific letters on the ground, identified using circles on a map, collecting letters that, once rearranged, will form the name of a European country. They may also use copies of the playground map to mark their own control points to give to another group.

PREPARATION

Using cones or markers, create four or five simple outline shapes on the ground outdoors, e.g. a rectangle, circle, square or triangle.

Tip: To avoid visual confusion, do this on plain surfaces, such as the field or an unmarked tarmac area.

Create a simple map to represent this on card (which can be laminated).

Resources

- Cones or markers arranged in shapes.
- Cards printed with a simple map (see example) to represent the outline shapes
- One enlarged copy of the map as a teaching aid
- Small counters (to be placed on the printed maps)
- Beanbags (small)

Previous learning

What do they already know about using maps?

CONSIDER

Health & Safety

Assess and evaluate hazards and risks in your setting. See the health and safety chapter.

LESSON OBJECTIVES

We are learning to identify where we are on a map.

National Curriculum Content

- Use fieldwork to observe human and physical features in the local area, using maps and plans.

ADULT ROLES

- Support the children to maintain the orientation of their maps as they follow a route.

WARM UP IDEAS

Explain that for the next six weeks the children will be exploring the school setting and surrounding area, using maps to find clues to help them develop their geographical knowledge.

How familiar are they with the outdoor learning area? Can they identify, name and describe human and physical geographical features in the learning area, e.g. grassed areas, parking areas, play areas, tarmac areas, walls, etc.? Could they confidently describe the setting to a partner?

Introductory activity

Cars: A blind trust game (in pairs)

Each child takes it in turns to be either the 'driver', with an imaginary steering wheel but with their eyes closed, or the 'backseat driver', who has their eyes open and their hands on the driver's shoulders.

The driver controls the speed but the backseat driver controls where they go, keeping them both safe and describing what they can see (geographical features) as they travel around the learning area.

Communicate feedback, discussing whether the descriptions were accurate and whether they felt safe, and what could have been done to make it an even better experience. Did they learn something new about the learning area?

MAIN ACTIVITIES

Where are we?

Working out position on a map (whole class and in pairs)

Explain that today the children will be learning how to use maps, using the shape zone of cones on the ground and a map of the area.

Set the enlarged map (see resources) on the floor, showing the children how to orientate it to the cones on the ground.

Identify the shapes on the ground and match them with those on the map.

Show the children how to move around the area and turn themselves but keep the map set (orientated) to the shapes on the ground.

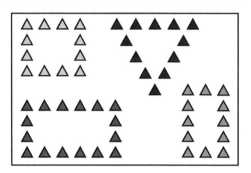

The adult points to their own position on the enlarged map, relating it to the shapes on the ground.

1. Ask one child to stand somewhere near the shapes on the ground. Can the children point to where that person is on their maps?
2. Ask the child to move to another point in the area. Can the children identify the new position on the map?
3. Can they use a finger to draw the route taken by the child?

Hand out the simple maps to pairs. They set their own maps to match the shape zone on the ground.

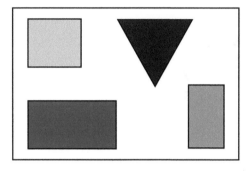

Challenge 1 (in pairs)

Identify where they are on a map

Children take it in turns to do the following tasks:

1. One person from each pair stands in the shape zone and their partner identifies their position on the map.
2. One person points to a point on the map and the partner goes to stand in that point in the shape zone.
3. One person places a counter on the map and the partner has to place a beanbag in the corresponding position on the shape zone.

4. One person places a beanbag in the shape zone and their partner places a counter on the corresponding point on the map.
5. In pairs, the children walk in the shape zone and identify where they are on the map. They draw their route with their fingers on the map.

Some children will find this easier if the shapes are colour-matched.

Some children will be able to draw and follow a route drawn on the map.

PLENARY

Encourage the children to explain what they have been doing in the session and state what they have found out about orientating a map, about human and physical geographical features in the area, and about trusting others to keep them safe.

Note: To reinforce the learning, provide an opportunity during free times (such as playtime) for the children to repeat the activity, drawing shapes on the ground and on a map of their own making, working with a partner to identify their position on the map or on the ground.

EVALUATION/FOLLOW ON

- What went well and why?
- What didn't go as well as expected?
- What could be changed?
- Who stood out and why?

PREPARATION

Make jigsaws by cutting up identical copies of a map of the world into eight pieces using straight cuts, with sufficient copies for one map per group.

Set out the shape zone as in Progression 1.

Prepare an arrows trail around the school grounds, using sticks, chalks, etc. and placing control point markers (e.g. recycled plastic containers) at key places for the children to find.

Place one piece of jigsaw per group in each container.

Mark out a 'river' using two ropes or sets of cones to form the banks.

Tip: To clearly identify the position of a control point, attach the containers to plastic fence posts or use brightly coloured ribbons.

Previous learning

Identify physical and human features on the school site, e.g. grassed areas, parking areas, play areas, tarmac areas, walls, etc.

Resources

- Cones and map of the shape zone from Progression 1
- Two small hoops, crates, rubber markers or wooden planks per group
- Map of the world cut up into an eight-piece jigsaw (one map per group)
- Eight containers to place the map pieces in, e.g. upcycled plastic containers
- Sticks or chalks for the arrows trail
- Clipboards, paper and pencils
- Basic map of the learning area

LESSON OBJECTIVES

We are following an arrows trail to collect parts of a world map jigsaw.

National Curriculum Content

- Locate the world's countries, using maps.
- Name and locate counties and cities of the UK.
- Use maps, atlases, globes and digital/computer mapping to locate countries.
- Use fieldwork to observe human and physical features in the local area.

ADULT ROLES

- Support the children to maintain the orientation of their maps as they follow a route.
- Model the activity.

WARM UP IDEAS

In the classroom before going out, use atlases and digital maps to identify the UK, the country, key cities, the county that the school is in, the surrounding counties and the county towns.

Zoom in to show the location of the school, identifying nearby human and physical geographical features. Are they familiar? Zoom in to the school and its grounds, identifying features within the setting. Does it match what they know? Are there any differences and why might this be? Why could they be different? Discuss changes over time.

Introductory activity

Defining and practising following an arrows trail

Explain that in this session the children will be following an arrows trail around the learning area. Have they followed an arrows trail before? Clarify the meaning of 'arrows trail', e.g. by using the shape zone from Progression 1 to follow a simple route around the shapes marked by arrows on the ground. Show what the arrows trail would look like on a map. Choose some volunteers to walk the arrows trail route. Can the children draw the route on their own maps?

CONSIDER

Health & Safety

Assess and evaluate hazards and risks in your setting. See the health and safety chapter.

MAIN ACTIVITIES

Arrows trail world map

Collect parts of a world map jigsaw to bring back to base to assemble

The children will follow trails of arrows marked by sticks or chalks on the ground, collecting parts of a jigsaw hidden in containers along the way in order to assemble the jigsaw at the end.

Show the children what the jigsaw pieces look like first, so they know what to look for, and remind them that they must take one jigsaw piece from each container. You could suspend the pieces above the ground. Highlighting the hiding places with brightly-coloured ribbon will help the children too.

Challenge 1 (in pairs or groups of four)

Follow the arrows trail, collecting controls

Starting groups at different points on the route, the children follow the arrows trail, collecting the controls (jigsaw pieces) from the control point containers.

When they have all eight pieces, they return to 'base' to assemble their jigsaw, identifying continents, countries and capital cities (if marked) using an atlas or digital technology to aid them.

- Can they locate the equator, the Tropics of Cancer and Capricorn and the Arctic and Antarctic Circles?

- Discuss the geographical, scientific and historical importance of these locations.

Challenge 2 (in pairs or groups of four)

Draw the arrows trail on the map to match features on the ground

Some children may be able to draw their own arrows trail on a basic map of the area, showing the route and its key features and identifying and naming human and physical geographical features in the learning area, e.g. grassed areas, parking areas, play areas, tarmac areas, walls, etc.

Some may represent these features with symbols and a key.

Optional extension (groups of four)

Cross the river

Explain that they are going to explore a geographical feature: a river. Is a river a human or physical geographical feature? What is a river? Where are rivers found and why are they important?

1. Each group lines up on one bank of the 'river'.

2. The task is to use the equipment (see resources) to cross the river, making sure that each team member crosses safely. The hoops act as stepping stones.
   - The hoops cannot be thrown or dragged, but can be picked up, moved and put down again.
   - The children do not all have to cross at the same time.
   - This is not a race. Which group can do it the most effectively and safely?

3. For more challenge, it can be done with one team member with their eyes closed or blindfolded or transporting a cup of vital 'medicine' (coloured water) across the river without spilling any of it.

4. Discuss what worked well and what could be improved another time.

PLENARY

Ask the children to explain what they have been doing and what they have found out about teamwork, communication, following a trail and the geography of the world. What do they know now that they did not know at the beginning of the session?

Back in the classroom

Research the location and importance of local or major rivers, investigating their ecology and how rivers benefit wildlife and flora.

EVALUATION/FOLLOW ON

- What went well and why?
- What didn't go as well as expected?
- What could be changed?
- Who stood out and why?

PREPARATION

Prepare the symbols cards, countries and capital cities cards (on different colour cards for each group).

Draw a map of the area, marking key features using symbols and keeping copies as masters for future activities.

Mark a map with the control points (use CP, numbers or letters) and an arrows trail showing the route to take.

Set out the trail with the control point containers in the relevant positions.

Resources

• Map symbol cards (see British Orienteering Tri-O Pages 20–28, available to download from www. britishorienteering.org.uk, and a cloth to cover them during Kim's game

• Map of the learning area marked with an arrows trail

• Ten cards (per group) marked with five countries and five corresponding capital cities

• Ten containers to place the map pieces in, e.g. upcycled plastic containers

• Atlases or digital maps

Previous learning

Has anyone visited a nearby river or another physical geographical feature?

CONSIDER

Health & Safety

Assess and evaluate hazards and risks in your setting. See the health and safety chapter.

LESSON OBJECTIVES

We are learning to follow a trail marked on a map, using arrows and symbols to collect the names of European countries and their capital cities.

National Curriculum Content

• Use maps to focus on Europe (countries and major cities).

• Use maps, atlases, globes and digital/computer mapping to locate countries and major cities.

• Use fieldwork to observe human and physical features in the local area.

ADULT ROLES

• Model the activity.

• Support the children with the positioning of features on maps.

• Reinforce and clarify the use of keys and symbols.

WARM UP IDEAS

Explain that this session the children will be following an arrows trail marked on a map of the area. But to make it really clear how to follow the trail, the map will have symbols to represent key features.

What is the purpose of the symbols? Can they name and give examples of human and physical geographical features in the learning area, e.g. grassed areas, play areas, tarmac areas, walls, etc.?

Introductory activity

Introducing map symbols playing 'Kim's game' (whole class and in pairs)

Standing in a circle, introduce the map symbols cards, discussing their meaning and matching with possible examples in the setting.

Use the cue cards to play 'Kim's game' (memory game).

1. Place the symbols in the centre of the circle and allow the children to look carefully at them for around 30 seconds.
2. Cover the symbols with a cloth or ask them to close their eyes and then tell a partner all the symbols they can remember. Uncover them and see whether they got them all.
3. Repeat but this time ask the children to close their eyes or look away while you remove one symbol.
4. Ask the children to open their eyes. Can they identify the missing one?

Europe and symbols map trail

Match map symbols to real examples in the setting

Explore the outdoor learning area, identifying key features and discussing how these could be marked on a map in the form of a symbol. Can they identify them as human or physical geographical features, e.g. grassed areas, trees, tarmac areas, walls, etc.?

Collect capital city and countries cards to bring back to the base to match

Point out that the arrows trail is marked on the map of the area and not on the ground this week.

Explain that their task is to look carefully on the map to see where the arrows trail goes, using the symbols indicating human and physical geographical features to help them to follow it.

They need to find and collect ten controls (five cards with the names of countries and five cards with the names of capital cities written on them) along the way, marked on the map as CP (control point).

Explain that they will be collecting cards of a particular colour, and assign a colour to each group.

Show an example of the controls and control point containers so that they know what to look for.

Emphasise that they must only take one piece – their colour - from each container.

Challenge 1 (groups of four)

Follow the arrows trail, collecting controls

Start groups at different points on the route to follow the arrows trail, collecting the controls (card pieces).

When they have all ten pieces, they return to 'base' to match their capital cities to the countries, using the atlases or digital technology to help them.

United Kingdom	London
France	Paris
Italy	Rome
Spain	Madrid
Portugal	Lisbon

Optional challenge 2 (in pairs)

Create their own arrows trail and draw a map for it, identifying key features on the ground using symbols (and providing a key)

1. The children create their own arrows trail for a partner, snapping or cutting lengths of twig to make directional arrows.

2. Their partner follows the trail.

3. Together, they draw a map to represent this trail, drawing symbols to represent key features and a key to interpret symbols.

4. Using their own arrows trail map, the children explore the area, perfecting their maps by adding additional features and adding these to the key.

5. This can then be given to another pair to try out.

Some children will need support to follow a trail or may need a peer leader or adult to support with the positioning of features on the map.

Some children may be able to link this to a science trail, identifying and naming trees, leaves and plants at each control point.

Encourage the children to explain what they have been doing in the session and state what they have found out about map trails, map symbols, European countries and capital cities.

- What went well and why?
- What didn't go as well as expected?
- What could be changed?
- Who stood out and why?

PREPARATION

Ensure that the outdoor learning area is clear of hazards.

Use the symbol cards from Progression 3 (with a few extra for more challenge if necessary).

Prepare basic maps of the setting area (without symbols).

Resources

- Two sets of map symbol cards – one card with the symbol and one card with the meaning (per group) – available from The British Orienteering Tri-O resource, pages 20–28
- Map key identification sheet, one per group
- Basic maps of the learning area without symbols
- Atlases or digital maps

Previous learning

Has anyone been on a journey since last week and used the satnav? Or drawn their own map?

CONSIDER

Health & Safety

Assess and evaluate hazards and risks in your setting. See the health and safety chapter.

LESSON OBJECTIVES

We are learning to make our own map of an area using arrows and symbols.

National Curriculum Content

- Use fieldwork to observe human and physical features in the local area.

ADULT ROLES

- Model the activity.
- Support with positioning of features.
- Clarify the use of key and symbols.

WARM UP IDEAS

Explain that today the children will be making their own arrows trail on a map of the area. But to make it really clear how to follow the map, they will use symbols to represent key features.

Introductory activity

Reinforcing map symbol recognition by playing 'Kim's game' relay (groups of four)

1. Lay the pairs of map symbols cards face down in a grid pattern – one grid per group.
2. The teams line up behind a line facing the grid pattern.
3. On the signal to start, the first person runs to the grid and turns over two map symbol cards.
4. If they match, e.g. the 'symbol for tree' and the word 'tree', then those two cards can be kept by the group. If they do not match, they are replaced face down (use a map key identification sheet to help).
5. The next person runs to the grid and turns over two cards.
6. If they match, they are kept; if they do not match, they are replaced face down on the grid.
7. The team must pay careful attention to the position of the cards so that they gradually learn the position of possible matching cards.
8. Then the rest of the team members have a go.
9. The aim is to be the first team to pick up all their cards.

This is a variation of Activity 3 (Matching Symbols) in the Tri-O British Orienteering resource, which contains printable copies of the map symbols cards and map key for this activity.

MAIN ACTIVITIES

Our area map

Revise and match map symbols to real examples

Explore the outdoor learning area, identifying key features, and revise how these could be marked on a map as symbols, identifying them as human or physical geographical features.

Model how to mark these on a basic map of the area, showing outlines of buildings and pathways, etc.

Challenge 1 (in pairs)

Create their own arrows trail, marking features using symbols

Using copies of the basic map of the area, tell the children that they will be drawing their own arrows trail for another pair to follow.

Start pairs at different points in the learning area to draw their own arrows trail on the basic map of the area, adding symbols at key features on their map.

Once complete, they walk their own trail, checking that it is accurate and adding more detail if necessary.

The groups then swap maps and try out a different map.

- How accurate is it? Why? Why not?
- Is it easy to follow? Why? Why not?

The pair that made the map makes improvements or adjustments.

Some children will need a peer leader or adult to support them to follow a trail or may need support with the positioning of features on the map.

Some children may be able to add more detail to their symbols, such as leaf shapes corresponding to species of trees found in the setting, or the site of a bug hotel, etc.

PLENARY

Encourage the children to explain what they have been doing in the session and state what they have found out about making and following maps.

In groups, play a game of symbols snap, matching the Tri-O map symbols.

EVALUATION/FOLLOW ON

- What went well and why?
- What didn't go as well as expected?
- What could be changed?
- Who stood out and why?

PREPARATION

On playground markings, e.g. a netball court, mark the letters of the alphabet in chalks.

Mark the position of letters on a master playground markings map, keeping a copy for reference purposes.

Draw arrows on a playground map to identify the positions of letters in the name of a European country – one map for each European country used (using different-coloured paper for each map can make it easier to identify which is which).

For more challenge, the letters can be scrambled and need to be unscrambled to make the name.

Label each map 1,2,3,4,5, etc., making a note of the name of the country corresponding to each map as an answer sheet.

Resources

- Playground labelled with letters of the alphabet (in chalks) and a cone to place on the ground to show the start of the route children will follow
- Five large copies of map number 1: start marked as ▲
- Copies of each 'European country' arrows trail map
- Copies of the playground markings map
- Copies of the master map and answers
- Clipboards, paper and pencils and playground chalks
- Maps and atlases of Europe

Previous learning

Has anyone been on a journey since last week, used the satnav or drawn their own map?

LESSON OBJECTIVES

We are learning to follow an arrows trail map to collect letters to make the names of European countries.

National Curriculum Content

- Locate the world's countries, using maps to focus on Europe.
- Use fieldwork to observe human features in the local area.

ADULT ROLES

- Model the activity.
- Support with orientating the maps.
- Verify the answers.

WARM UP IDEAS

Explain that today's lesson will be on the playground.

Walk the group along the playground markings lines, 'following the leader' to explore the chalk-marked letters. What are they? Where are they placed? Point out that some letters are on one side of a line and others are on the other side of a line. What do the children think they will be used for?

Introductory activity

Balance on the line

For a more physical warm up, use the lines as markers to stop on, do exercises and balance on.

1. The children jog around the playground in different directions.
2. On a command signal such as a whistle, they stop then run to the nearest line and balance in a way called out by the teacher, e.g. balanced on tiptoes, balanced on heels, one heel one toe, balanced on one foot, balanced with only one foot and one hand on the line, balanced in the shape of a letter C or X, etc.

CONSIDER

Health & Safety

Assess and evaluate hazards and risks in your setting. See the health and safety chapter.

MAIN ACTIVITIES

Arrows trail and countries' names

Observe how to orientate a map of the playground (whole class)

Using the enlarged copies of map number 1, point out the start position marked on the map by the triangle and on the ground by the cone.

Model how to move around the playground keeping the map in line with the markings on the ground, following the arrows on the map to each letter in turn.

Explain that when collected, the letters make up the name of a European country.

Their task will be to follow the arrows trail on each map to collect letters on their paper (on a clipboard) to spell the name of a European country. They can use atlases to help them to do this.

- When they have the European country name, they take the number of their map and their answer to an adult, who tells them whether it is correct or not (the spelling must be correct).

- If it is correct, they can choose another map to find another country.

- If it is not correct, then they must repeat that trail again to check their route.

To make this a more challenging activity, the letters can be scrambled, so that the pairs or groups have to work together to unscramble the letters to make the name of the country.

Challenge 1 (in pairs)

Use arrows trail maps to collect letters to spell the name of European countries

Pairs complete the task as described above.

Some individuals may need support to follow the arrows trail or need a peer leader or adult to support with orientating the map, identifying the correlating positions shown by the arrows.

Optional extension

Some children may be able to draw their own arrows trails to give to another group to complete.

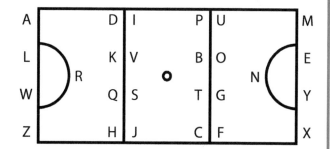

PLENARY

Encourage the children to explain what they have been doing in the session and state what they have found out about following arrows on a map and any new countries that they have found.

Leave the chalk marks on the ground for the children to practise or use during playtimes.

EVALUATION/FOLLOW ON

- What went well and why?
- What didn't go as well as expected?
- What could be changed?
- Who stood out and why?

PREPARATION

On playground markings, e.g. a netball court, mark the letters of the alphabet in chalks, as in Progression 5.

Use the master copy map of the playground from Progression 5.

Draw circles on a playground markings map to identify the positions of letters in the name of a European country – one map for each country used (using different colours for each map makes them easier to identify).

Label each map 1,2,3,4,5, etc., making a note of the name of the country corresponding to each map on an answer sheet.

Resources

- Ropes or tubular webbing (for the introductory activity)

- Playground labelled with letters of the alphabet and a cone to place on the ground to show the start of the route children will follow

- Five large copies of map number 1: mark the start of the route with a triangle.

- Copies of each European country map with the position of each letter in the name marked by a circle

- Copies of the playground markings map

- Copies of the master map and answers

- Clipboards, paper and pencils and playground chalks

- Maps and atlases of the world

Previous learning

Has anyone used the playground markings during playtime to make a map?

LESSON OBJECTIVES

We are learning to follow a map to collect letters which spell the names of European countries..

National Curriculum Content

- Locate the world's countries, using maps to focus on Europe.

- Use fieldwork to observe human features in the local area.

ADULT ROLES

- Model the activity and verify the answers.

- Support with orientating the maps.

WARM UP IDEAS

Explain that today's session will again take place on the playground. Walk the group along the playground markings lines, following the leader to revise the chalk-marked letters.

Introductory activity

Inclusive circles game

Explain that this challenge is about leaving groups and joining other groups.

1. Make five or six large circles on the ground using ropes or tubular webbing and ask the children to stand in one of the circles.

2. Decide on a category, e.g. the tallest person. The tallest person in each group (decided by the group) must leave the group with a wave goodbye.

3. They are now free to choose another group to join, who can encourage them to join by calling out 'over here, join us', etc.

4. The aim of the challenge is to encourage as many people as possible to join your group.

5. Other categories could include: who has the most brothers and sisters, who has the biggest feet, who has the longest hair, who has visited the most countries, who has travelled the furthest, etc. Consider what it feels like to leave a group then be welcomed by another group.

CONSIDER

Health & Safety

Assess and evaluate hazards and risks in your setting. See the health and safety chapter.

Playground markings orienteering and European country names

Revise how to orientate a map of the playground

Using the enlarged copies of map number 1, point out the start position marked on the map by the triangle and on the ground by the cone, and how the points are now marked with circles. What difference will this make, i.e. that they can be visited in any order? What is the impact of this?

Revise how to move around the playground keeping the map in line with the markings on the ground, addressing any difficulties that were experienced in Progression 5, and this time going to the points on the map marked with circles.

Observe how to identify circled control points on a map to collect information

Point out that this time the points on the map are marked with circles. What might this mean, e.g. the letters may be out of spelling order? They can use atlases to help them to unscramble the words.

- When they have the European country name, they will need to take the number of their map and their answer to an adult, who tells them whether it is correct or not (the spelling must be correct).

- If it is correct, they can choose another map to find another country.

- If it is not correct then they must repeat that trail again to check their route, identifying where they went wrong.

Adults can support those finding it difficult by providing the first letter.

Challenge 1 (in pairs)

Use circled points to collect letters to spell names of European countries

Pairs complete the task as described above.

Extension

Some children may be able to draw their own circles map identifying a different country, to give to another group to complete.

Encourage the children to explain what they have been doing in the session and state what they have found out about finding positions on a map and any new countries that they have learned. Was it more challenging, and how were these challenges overcome?

Think back to the warm up activity. How did it feel to leave a group and then decide which group to join? What influenced their choices? Why is this? What might they do differently next time?

- What went well and why?
- What didn't go as well as expected?
- What could be changed?
- Who stood out and why?

History

In this unit, children will be exploring the Victorian period, often through the eyes of the botanist and artist Beatrix Potter. She had a natural instinct to sketch and tell stories about everything she loved. Each week, the children will work historically by learning about a particular theme during the Victorian era, followed by what Beatrix Potter did in comparison, and ultimately gain a fun insight into the tale of Peter Rabbit and his animal friends. They will be challenged to develop their outdoor learning skills, heightening their awareness of natural surroundings and appreciating and forming a love of flora and fauna through immersive activities, e.g. sensory trails and sketching plants and animals, and will develop their personal creativity.

To support inclusive practice or to extend learning, the space, task, equipment and people (STEP) approach can be adopted throughout this unit. By changing the space, task, equipment or people, the activity can be made more challenging or easier to understand, enabling all pupils to take part in the activity, as explained in the assessment chapter in this book.

The main activities offer opportunities for adult-directed whole-group and smaller-group work, as well as opportunities for individual exploration and experimentation where appropriate. Timings will vary according to your setting, pupil experience and the support available. The children will be expected to work independently or together in small groups with support from an adult, as described in each progression.

You may wish to record the activities using a camera.

Natural connections

- Observation of natural materials
- Creative designs with nature
- Paying close attention to the natural world
- Reflecting on our relationship with animals and plants.

Health and wellbeing

- Physical activity
- Creativity
- Teamwork
- Self-regulation and independence
- Risk-management
- Emotional resilience.

Word bank

The Victorian era

- Queen Victoria
- blackboard
- slate
- hopscotch
- women's roles
- laundry

'Inky' Stephens

- invention of blue-black ink

Brunel

- railway
- bridges
- brass
- steel

Beatrix Potter

- Peter Rabbit
- camomile
- velvet
- Herdwick sheep
- Lake District

Summary overview

Progression	Curriculum content	Learning experiences/activities
Lesson 1	To study the Victorians in British history, to extend pupils' chronological knowledge.	Produce a timeline of significant events throughout history, including the introduction of the Victorian era. Experience an immersion of Queen Victoria's life in an outdoor space. Who was Beatrix Potter? Investigate what it would be like to have grown up as a Victorian woman. Read *The Tale of Peter Rabbit*. Invitation to a Peter Rabbit tea party with currant buns, and experience camomile tea using a storm kettle.
Lesson 2	To recognise a significant turning point in British history.	Build a bridge to support weight and compare to the engineering landmarks of the Victorian era, e.g. Isambard Kingdom Brunel's Clifton Suspension Bridge. Appreciate Beatrix Potter's life and achievements in challenging times. Read *The Tale of Squirrel Nutkin* (Beatrix Potter produced 23 original tales).
Lesson 3	To understand the differences between a Victorian and present-day child.	Understand Queen Victoria's family tree and create a family tree with sticks. Experience Victorian children's games and walk tall with a feather beneath your chin! Make your own hopscotch. Read *The Tale of Mrs Tiggy-Winkle*. Think about living as a Victorian woman and learning to do the laundry.
Lesson 4	To acknowledge how Victoria has shaped this nation and the impact that Beatrix Potter had within it.	Leisure time for Victoria. Observation and sketches of flora and fauna. Set up a sensory trail, including textures and smells found in *The Tale of Peter Rabbit* e.g. lavender, cotton, fur, velvet, camomile and brass buttons.
Lesson 5	To comprehend how Victorians influenced and were influenced by the wider world.	Hands-on drawing from nature, whatever the weather! Make your own nature paintbrush. Extension: Using the Japanese art of *tataki zome*, pound natural pigment into cloth to create a beautiful work of art.
Lesson 6	To understand historical concepts such as continuity and change.	Demonstrate the incredible selection of children's books produced during the Victorian era, e.g. *Alice in Wonderland* and *The Jungle Book*. Create a storyboard of a tale. Look at Henry 'Inky' Stephens – the inventor of blue-black ink. Look at Beatrix Potter's legacy: the National Trust and protection of the Herdwicks.

PREPARATION

Write each event listed on page 75 on a separate wooden disc, without its date. Gather photographs of Victoria growing up and enjoying hobbies.

Collect old frames to frame the images or laminate them, so they can be placed outdoors in the learning area.

Make invitations to a Peter Rabbit tea party for the class.

Resources

- Beatrix Potter's *The Tale of Peter Rabbit*
- *Miss Potter* film
- Camomile tea, water, storm kettle, teapot, fire steel and fuel
- Currant buns and napkins
- Plastic shot glasses for camomile tea taster
- Wood slices with holes or alternative decorations

Previous learning

Introduce some significant events that happened during the Victorian era in the classroom before the first progression outside.

CONSIDER

Health & Safety

Assess and evaluate hazards and risks in your setting. See the health and safety chapter.

LESSON OBJECTIVES

We are gaining an understanding of the incredible Victorian era: what happened, what was made and built and how Beatrix Potter lived her life during that time.

National Curriculum Content

- To study the Victorians in British history, to extend pupils' chronological knowledge.

ADULT ROLES

- Either to assist the teacher or to lead a group.

WARM UP IDEAS

Play a game of 'Line up', where each pair has a wooden disc with a significant event during the Victorian era, as listed on page 75. Can the class reorder themselves into a timeline, recreating the timeline from prior learning and learning in the moment?

Introductory activity (whole class and in pairs)

Understanding the journey of Victoria's life

Victoria was born at Kensington Palace, London, in 1819. Although she had a strict and lonely upbringing, Victoria was a lively and intelligent girl who enjoyed painting, riding, music, singing and dancing. Children should immerse themselves in the history of Victoria by looking at the photographs of her life presented in the outdoor learning area. With a partner, they ask each other key questions about the photographs in turn to develop their knowledge. For example:

- How old was Victoria when she became queen?
- How many children did Victoria and Albert have?
- Which Christmas tradition did Victoria and Albert introduce to Britain?
- What was the name of the museum that opened in 1852?

Add questions for an interactive display that can be changed to answers as the progression in learning goes on.

MAIN ACTIVITIES

Queen Victoria, Beatrix Potter and a well-loved bunny

Challenge 1 (individual)

Peter Rabbit's tea party invitations

Hand out rough invitations on card to attend Peter Rabbit's tea party. The card invite could include a title, place, date, time and RSVP. The children add an illustration to the invitation. They then swap their invitation with a peer.

Challenge 2 (whole class)

Making camomile tea

In the fire-lighting area, discuss how to make camomile tea for the tea party. Children should find thin and medium sticks. Children gather fuel for the storm kettle and sort fuel into two piles. Talk about how important planning and preparation is in fire-lighting. Pour water into the kettle. The teacher should ignite the fire in the base of the storm kettle (refer to the health and safety chapter) and ask individual children to come up to the storm kettle and feed the fire. Keep the fire going until steam is seen. Make and hand out the camomile tea tasters and currant buns.

Challenge 3 (whole class)

Tea party time!

Explain how the Victorians enjoyed afternoon tea! Set the tea party atmosphere with a reading from *The Tale of Peter Rabbit*. Talk about what you notice during the story. What can we find out about life in Victorian times from this story?

Some events in the Victoria era

24 May 1819 – Victoria born

1837 – Victoria became queen

1840 – 5,000 miles of railway track were laid

1840 – First Christmas tree introduced by Albert

1843 – Brunel's SS Great Britain transatlantic launch

1843 – *A Christmas Carol* by Charles Dickens and first Christmas cards were sold

1851 – Great Exhibition at Crystal Palace

1852 – The Victoria and Albert museum opened

1864 – Brunel's Clifton Suspension Bridge opened

1866 – Beatrix Potter born

1880 – The Education Act decreed that all children aged five to ten had to go to school

22 January 1901 – Queen Victoria died

1902 – *The Tale of Peter Rabbit* published

PLENARY

Go around the fire-lighting area and ask each child to share some of the history of the Victorian era, how to use a storm kettle safely or what they remember about the Peter Rabbit story. Identify the key points the children raise so that they will be helped to recall their knowledge and understanding when the next opportunity arises.

Back in the classroom

- Study the Victorian era. Look at the timeline and ask children to record it in their books.

- Start watching the *Miss Potter* film and discuss how life was different during Victorian times.

EVALUATION/FOLLOW ON

- What went well and why?
- What could be improved?
- What could be changed?
- Who stood out and why?
- How can you display the children's work in class?
- What have the children enjoyed?

PREPARATION

Build a model bridge and raft beforehand.

Collect and laminate pictures of Brunel's Clifton Suspension Bridge.

Review http://www.ikbrunel. org.uk/clifton-suspension-bridge.

Resources

- Pictures of the Clifton Suspension Bridge
- Beatrix Potter's *A Journal* and *The Tale of Squirrel Nutkin*
- Knots, sticks, air-dry clay and twine
- Large, flat container to hold water for raft-floating test

Previous learning

Read *The Tale of Squirrel Nutkin* in class and discuss.

CONSIDER

Health & Safety

Assess and evaluate hazards and risks in your setting. See the health and safety chapter.

LESSON OBJECTIVES

We are building a bridge using sticks and clay and a raft using traditional lashing techniques and reflecting on a great Victorian engineer. We are listening and gaining an insight into what Beatrix Potter achieved during her lifetime.

National Curriculum Content

- To recognise a significant turning point in British history.

ADULT ROLES

- Either to assist the teacher or to lead a group.

WARM UP IDEAS

Take a tour of the school grounds or local neighbourhood. What things can the children spot that have been invented? Can they estimate when these were invented – which century? Are any Victorian? The school building itself might be Victorian, as The Education Act in 1880 decreed that all children aged five to ten had to go to school. If there is a railway nearby, talk about the 'railway boom' of the 1840s, when thousands of miles of track were laid in Britain. Talk about the great Isambard Kingdom Brunel and his influence on railways, revolutionising transport of goods and people. Talk about the differences between natural and manufactured. Do they know of any inventors?

Introductory activity

In recognition of Beatrix Potter's life and achievements, share readings from Beatrix Potter's *A Journal*. Select appropriate sections of writing to share and discuss the key achievements of Beatrix Potter during the Victorian era. Compare her life as a woman to that of Brunel as a man.

MAIN ACTIVITIES

Inventions from the past and present

Challenge 1 (in groups of four)

Build a bridge using sticks and clay

Study pictures of Brunel's Clifton Suspension Bridge. In teams of three or four, discuss how you will make your bridge. Collect sticks and present your final design in 2D, i.e. laying it on the ground. If successful, the team will be rewarded with a handful of clay to turn the 2D bridge into 3D!

Challenge 2 (whole class and groups of four)

Planning rafts

Listen again to *The Tale of Squirrel Nutkin* and plan how to create a model raft which floats. Model the skill of a clove hitch knot and how to make the frame for the raft using square lashing. (See www.bloomsbury.com/NC-Outdoors). Allow time for children to talk about what they need for the raft and how to share the tasks amongst them.

Challenge 3 (groups of four)

Build and launch a Squirrel Nutkin raft with a squirrel model made from air-dry clay to test it out

Children collaborate to build the raft they planned in Challenge 2 as well as a small squirrel from a lump of clay. How will they ensure that the raft will float? How will the squirrel balance on the raft? Talk about roles: the inventors, engineers, the sculptors and the clients, linking to design and technology product evaluation. Allow time for each group to conduct a test of their product and make any changes as a result of their tests.

PLENARY

Set up a gallery of bridges. Give children the opportunity to share their thoughts and ideas about who has the strongest bridge design and why. What modern bridges do they know of? How do they compare?

Present a gallery of Squirrel Nutkin rafts. Did all the rafts float? Which raft could be taken on the longest journey? What were the main challenges and how did they overcome these?

EVALUATION/FOLLOW ON

- What went well and why?
- What could be improved?
- What could be changed?
- Who stood out and why? How can you display the children's work in class?
- What have the children enjoyed?

Back in the classroom

- Continue to watch the *Miss Potter* film and discuss what inventions are apparent during the film and what you have talked about to date as having been invented during Victorian times.

- Ask children to research a particular invention of the period and write about it to contribute to the classroom display. Add images of the bridges they built to the display.

PREPARATION

Set up the outdoor learning area ready for the washing task (Challenge 3).

Write each name of Victoria's family (see Challenge 1) on a different wood slice.

Resources

- Books light and small enough for children to place on their heads
- *The Tale of Mrs Tiggy-Winkle* by Beatrix Potter
- Blindfolds
- Selection of objects
- Sticks and around 20 wood slices
- Feathers or similar
- Tubs, soap, water, dirty washing(!), dolly pegs and washing line

Previous learning

In class, look up Queen Victoria's family tree and sketch it out or print a copy to use as a reference outside.

Read *The Tale of Mrs Tiggy-Winkle*. Discuss living as a Victorian woman and learning to do the laundry.

CONSIDER

Health & Safety

Assess and evaluate hazards and risks in your setting. See the health and safety chapter.

LESSON OBJECTIVES

We are gaining knowledge about Victoria's family tree and experiencing and understanding some of the games Victorian children would have played in comparison to modern times. We are realising that it was expected that many women would spend whole days washing clothes, linen and bedding!

National Curriculum Content

- To understand the differences between a Victorian and present-day child.

ADULT ROLES

- Either to assist the teacher or to lead a group.

WARM UP IDEAS

Play party games from Victoria's era. Compare and contrast to modern times – what games do the children play at birthday parties? Explain that adults would also play these, as there were no TVs in homes.

- Blind man's buff: Blindfold one of the children, and the other children have a zoned area to move in. The blindfolded child is spun around and then must try to catch someone. When someone is caught, the blindfolded child must identify who they have caught. If not, play continues.

- Kim's game: A tray or similar is prepared with a selection of small items, e.g. items from a rucksack to take on an expedition or items needed for starting a fire. The tray is covered. The children compile a list of the objects. How many can they remember?

- Hopscotch: Mark out a hopscotch grid on the playground or with sticks.

Introductory activity (in pairs)

Explain that learning to be a queen for Victoria would have involved learning to walk, talk and act like royalty.

In pairs, children practise walking tall with books on their heads, arm in arm. How far can they go? Put a rope along the ground as a finish line and challenge three or four pairs. Queen Victoria may have practised with a string of holly leaves around her neck! How tricky is it to walk with a book on your head and a feather beneath your chin (not so prickly!)?

MAIN ACTIVITIES

A Victorian childhood

These can be done sequentially or as a carousel of activities, supported by other adults.

Challenge 1 (whole class, in pairs and groups)

Create Victoria's family tree with sticks and wood slices

Prepare the main stem of the family tree using sticks. Decide together how many branches will be needed for the Victoria and Albert family tree – their parents, themselves and their children.

Referring to copies of the researched family tree, children in pairs then select a wooden disc with the name of a member of Victoria's family and place it on the correct level of the family tree, discussing what their relationship is to Victoria.

- Victoria Duchess of Kent (Victoria's mother) and Edward Duke of Kent (Victoria's father).

- Princess Louise of Saxe-Gotha-Altenberg (Albert's mother) and Ernest I Duke of Saxe-Coburg and Gotha (Albert's father).

- Then Queen Victoria and Prince Albert

- The final tier comprises nine twigs to include Victoria and Albert's children: Victoria, Albert, Alice, Alfred, Helena, Louise, Arthur, Leopold and Beatrice.

Challenge 2 (in pairs)

Make a dolly peg doll using scraps of material and draw the features

Victoria and Beatrix would have played games as children, indoors and outdoors.

Most Victorian toys were made of materials such as wood, fabric, china or metal. Poor Victorian children usually had homemade toys, e.g. clothes peg dolls and skipping ropes. Wealthy children owned manufactured toys, e.g. rocking horses, dolls and clockwork train sets. Make a dolly peg doll using scraps of material and draw the features. (Sawn lengths of stick with a whittled area for the face could also be used.)

Challenge 3 (in pairs)

Have a go at washing some clothes by hand!

Reread *The Tale of Mrs Tiggy-Winkle* and discuss how washing is done at home now and by whom. Prepare tubs of water, soap and a washing line with dolly pegs. Can the children wash an item of clothing and hang it on the washing line? What does this feel like? Can they imagine spending a whole day doing the whole family's clothes (with people not changing them very often, so they were very dirty!)? How long will it take for the clothes to dry?

PLENARY

Reflect on how differently the Victorians lived day to day to how we do. A Victorian woman was expected to behave and do certain jobs. How are jobs divided in homes nowadays?

Back in the classroom

- Continue to watch *Miss Potter* and discuss the difference between children today and how children were then.

- Write about children now and then. Children could record this in their books using photographs and illustrations.

EVALUATION/FOLLOW ON

- What went well and why?
- What could be improved?
- What could be changed?
- Who stood out and why?
- How can you display the children's work in class?
- What have the children enjoyed?

PREPARATION

Set up the sensory trail in the outdoor learning area.

Resources

- Sensory trail items, e.g. lavender, cotton squares, cotton wool (pretend rabbit fur), velvet squares, camomile flowers or brass buttons
- Clipboards, paper and pencils for whole class

Previous learning

The progression will draw on the English progressions, exploring the senses.

Discuss leisure time for Victoria and ladies in Victorian times and what it was like for the working classes.

CONSIDER

Health & Safety

Assess and evaluate hazards and risks in your setting. See the health and safety chapter.

LESSON OBJECTIVES

We are considering the hobbies that Victoria and Beatrix Potter enjoyed with their children and developing the skill of drawing either flora or fauna. We are remembering the story of Peter Rabbit and reliving the tale by becoming immersed in a sensory trail incorporating significant strands of the story.

National Curriculum Content

- To acknowledge how Victoria shaped this nation and the impact that Beatrix Potter had within it.

ADULT ROLES

- Either to assist the teacher or to lead a group.

WARM UP IDEAS

Encourage the children to explore and find a special place. Ask the children to take time to look at this space and remember it. Closely note its features. They may use this space to do a sketch later in the lesson.

Introductory activity (whole class and in pairs)

Explain that Victoria would work during the mornings, pinpointing the key decisions that she made about her country, but that she would then have leisure time. Talk about the activities that Victoria and Beatrix may perhaps have enjoyed in their leisure time, e.g. walking, riding, drawing and painting.

Take the children on a walk in pairs around the local neighbourhood. Ask the children to talk with their partner about what they would enjoy doing in their own time and how it is different from what they might do as Victorian children. You could also point out any Victorian buildings or go to a park established in Victorian times and ask them to imagine what it would be like to have horses and carriages instead of cars.

MAIN ACTIVITIES

Exploring the outdoor learning area

Challenge 1 (in pairs)

Sensory trail based on *The Tale of Peter Rabbit*

Place items related to the plot of *The Tale of Peter Rabbit* in tins or baskets, scattered around the outdoor space. Each pair collects a sample of each item to demonstrate that they visited each area. On return to the gathering point, children identify where the items appear in the story of Peter Rabbit and reorder the items. Can they retell the story once they are happy with the order?

Challenge 2 (individual)

Observe and sketch flora and fauna as Beatrix Potter did so often

Invite the children to revisit their special spot with a clipboard, paper and pencil, to sketch something natural that is interesting and special to them.

If the school has pet animals, it may be possible to do some observational sketches.

PLENARY

Children remind each other of what the five senses are: sight, touch, smell, hearing and taste. What senses did they use today? For example, hearing cars; looking carefully at natural and built objects; touching the surfaces of natural and man-made objects. Did they use their sense of smell and taste? What smells and tastes might have been present in Victorian times? What did the children find today on the sensory trail and what part did it play in *The Tale of Peter Rabbit*? Can a group volunteer to act out the story using the sensory trail objects that have been put in order of when they appear in the story?

EVALUATION/FOLLOW ON

- What went well and why?
- What could be improved?
- What could be changed?
- Who stood out and why?
- How can you display the children's work in class?
- What have the children enjoyed?

Back in the classroom

- Continue to watch *Miss Potter* and study the way she worked, using her bedroom as her studio and her sketchbook 'out in the field'.

- Having completed sketches outdoors, children produce a watercolour painting from their favourite sketch. These could contribute to a display about Beatrix Potter's books.

PREPARATION

Make your own natural paintbrush.

Review www.indiaflint.com/ecoprint

and

https://kindlingplayandtraining.co.uk/crafts-and-projects/hapa-zome-beating-up-leaves-with-hammers.

Resources

- Twine or craft wire
- Smooth, hand-sized pebbles
- Cloth pieces for *tataki zome*
- Log slices
- Cartridge paper, watercolour paints and paintbrushes
- Clipboards – enough for whole class

CONSIDER

Health & Safety

Assess and evaluate hazards and risks in your setting. See the health and safety chapter.

LESSON OBJECTIVES

We are spending time outdoors in nature. We are being still, quiet and reflective. We are creating our own nature's paintbrush, a watercolour painting and some *tataki zome*!

National Curriculum Content

- To comprehend how Victorians influenced and were influenced by the wider world.

ADULT ROLES

- Either to assist the teacher or to lead a group.

WARM UP IDEAS

Discuss what pummelling is, i.e. striking repeatedly. Each child is given or finds a suitable pummelling pebble to hold. They need to be small enough to hold securely but big enough so that fingers are clear of the ground when knocked against it. To practise the skill of pummelling, ask the children to copy the technique at the same time as the teacher. The teacher bangs out a rhythm and the children copy it. Depending on the group, children may be able to create a pattern of sounds with the pebbles on the ground that the rest of the class copy.

Introductory activity

Showing, exploring and comparing Beatrix Potter's art with *tataki zome* art

Tataki zome is the Japanese art of bashing leaves and petals with hammers, pounding natural pigments into cloth. You may have heard it called 'hapa zome', a name coined by an Australian artist who had not realised this Japanese technique already had a name. What differences do they notice between this method and Beatrix Potter's style of art?

MAIN ACTIVITIES

The paintbrush in nature

Challenge 1 (individual)

Create your own natural paintbrush

Collect a pencil-sized stick. Find suitable natural materials to create the brush. It may be a leaf or a collection of grasses. Wrap the 'brush' around the pencil stick and tie with twine, or use craft wire for a quicker/user-friendly alternative.

Challenge 2 (individual)

Use your own paintbrush to add watercolour to paper

How well does your paintbrush work? Can you make a special effect? How would you change the brush to get a different pattern? Compare and contrast with a brush that Beatrix Potter was likely to use.

Challenge 3 (individual)

Try the Japanese art of *tataki zome* to produce a picture of nature

Collect flowers, petals and leaves beforehand but also allow the children to walk around their wild space and collect fallen flowers, petals and leaves from the ground (fresh, juicy ones are best as they give more colour). Choose a wooden disc, a piece of cloth, a smooth rock and your chosen collection of flora to prepare for *tataki zome*. Arrange the flora on half of the cloth on top of a log slice, either in a pattern or creating a picture. Fold the 'empty' half of cloth over the top and pummel the rock over and over on top to imprint the cloth with colour!

PLENARY

Have a tour of the outdoor gallery, including nature's paintbrushes, watercolour paintings and *tataki zome* art. Return to the gathering point and become an art critic. Talk to the child next to you and discuss your favourite art piece and why. Consider how Beatrix Potter would sketch in all weathers but how her pencil and watercolour sketches are very different from the *tataki zome* method. What reasons for the different approaches might there be?

EVALUATION/FOLLOW ON

- What went well and why?
- What could be improved?
- What could be changed?
- Who stood out and why?
- How can you display the children's work in class?
- What have the children enjoyed?

Back in the classroom

- Continue to watch *Miss Potter* and identify her strength of character in continuing with her stories and sketches. Discuss when children have felt determined.

- Introduce some of Beatrix Potter's other passions besides sketching, e.g. maintaining 4,000 acres of land and protecting the Herdwick breed of sheep.

PREPARATION

Collect children's classic books from the library.

Optional: Collect and make oak gall ink and source traditional blue/black ink.

Collect pebbles and source merino wool.

Review/record www.youtube.com/watch?v=y7k4-wj8mZ8, www.nationaltrust.org.uk/beatrix-potter-gallery-and-hawkshead/features/beatrix-potter-the-farmer, https://crafts.tutsplus.com/tutorials/fundamentals-of-wet-felting--cms-20738 and www.bbc.co.uk/radio4/history/making_history/makhist10_prog11b.shtml.

Resources

- Victorian children's books, e.g. *Alice's Adventures in Wonderland* and *Through the Looking Glass*, *The Tale of Peter Rabbit*, *Treasure Island*, *The Jungle Book*, *Black Beauty*.
- Feathers (to use as quills)
- Optional: Pre-prepared oak gall ink and traditional ink, iron sulphate (bought from a garden centre) and cartridge paper
- Picture of a Herdwick sheep
- Pebbles, merino wool (black, white, grey and brown), washing up liquid, water and netting
- Clipboards, paper and pencils

Previous learning

Talk about Henry 'Inky' Stephens – the inventor of blue-black ink.

Let children look at the library of Victorian children's books before going outside.

LESSON OBJECTIVES

We are becoming absorbed by classic children's literature written during the Victorian era. We are learning and understanding how oak gall ink is made and using it in storytelling.

We are making a wet felting 'sheep' pebble.

National Curriculum Content

- To understand historical concepts such as continuity and change.

ADULT ROLES

- Either to assist the teacher or to lead a group.

WARM UP IDEAS

Play a jungle game: 'Sleeping lions'. Children have to lie down absolutely still, as if they move, they are 'out'. One or two children try to make them wake up. What classic story is set in a jungle?

Introductory activity

Having created some oak gall ink beforehand, demonstrate making oak gall ink using a step-by-step procedure.

1. Crush oak galls with mortar and pestle.
2. Pour rainwater over the oak galls, stir and leave to soak for 24 hours.
3. Strain the mixture through a coffee filter.
4. Add some iron sulphate and stir to produce oak gall ink.

Note: This could be done inside before the progression outside, or the children could instead watch a video of the process (see the Resources section).

CONSIDER

Health & Safety

Assess and evaluate hazards and risks in your setting. See the health and safety chapter.

MAIN ACTIVITIES

A storyteller and environmentalist

Challenge 1 (in pairs and groups of four)

Dramatise a storyboard idea and complete a story of your own influenced by the Beatrix Potter tales

In pairs, discuss what the story might be about and what happens. Choose six different scenes or pages for the story and sketch them on pieces of paper. For example:

- You could choose a different animal dressed up in the first frame.

- Show a problem or adventure that this animal might have for the next frame.

- The third frame might show who helps the animal.

- The fourth might be what they do together.

- The fifth might show the problem solved.

- The sixth might end with them being comfy in the animal's home.

Re-enact the story with your partner and perform to another pair. One child is the narrator and one is the performer. The watching pair is the audience first and then performs to the others.

Challenge 2 (in pairs)

Victorian handwriting

Remind the children about 'Inky' Stephens. From the fifth to the nineteenth century (an incredible period of time), iron gall ink was used before the invention of blue and black ink.

Children should decide and write the title of their tale using a feather quill with oak gall ink or blue/black ink.

Take turns to write a sentence from your story. How does it feel to try to write neatly with a quill? They were used until the middle of the nineteenth century, when steel nibs became mass-produced. These were dipped into an inkwell like a quill, until the idea of a fountain pen with an internal reservoir of ink began, also in the nineteenth century.

Challenge 3 (whole class and in pairs)

Wet felting sheep

Listen to the incredible achievement that Beatrix Potter made towards the protection of the Herdwicks. 95 percent of the Herdwick sheep population can be found within 25 km of Coniston in the Lake District, according to the Sheep Trust.

Create a wet felting pebble as a reminder of the Herdwicks in the Lake District. Follow the step-by-step instructions as listed in the resources and previously prepared for reference outside.

PLENARY

Can children recall and briefly retell a children's classic from the Victorian era? Are there any things they notice about the Victorian children's tales? Are the stories still relevant to us today?

Beatrix Potter helped to preserve Lake District farms from unsuitable development in the early part of the twentieth century by preserving thousands of acres of land now protected by the National Trust. She played a major part in the conservation of the Herdwick breed. Why is it important to conserve nature and rare breeds? Talk about biodiversity and our connection to the natural world. Do Beatrix Potter's animals/humans, like Peter Rabbit, help us to care for nature?

Back in the classroom

- Complete watching *Miss Potter*.

- Discuss her life and achievements and how life was different and the same as today in Victorian times.

- Encourage the children to complete a timeline of key Victorian events they have learned about for the classroom display.

EVALUATION/FOLLOW ON

- What went well and why?

- What could be improved?

- What could be changed?

- Who stood out and why?

- How can you display the children's work in class?

- What have the children enjoyed?

- What have they achieved through this unit?

Art and Design

Based on the Key Stage 2 art and design objectives identified in the 2014 National Curriculum for England, in this unit children develop their understanding of 'place and space' through an exploration of colour, pattern, texture, line and the effect of light on objects to replicate shape and form in the context of the natural environment. Illustrations from a variety of children's books linked to nature are used as starting points to introduce visual arts terminology and to demonstrate creative use of different techniques and materials. The children experiment with these techniques and materials, demonstrating increasing control in creating their own artworks in a variety of media, learning to decide how (and for whom) they should be presented. There are links to Year 3 science National Curriculum content (plants, rocks and light).

To support inclusive practice or to extend learning, the space, task, equipment and people (STEP) approach can be adopted throughout this unit. By changing the space, task, equipment or people, the activity can be made more challenging or easier to understand, enabling all pupils to take part in the activity, as explained in the assessment chapter in this book.

The children will be expected to work as a whole group directed by the teacher, together in small groups of two to four with support from adults, and independently. The role of the adult is to lead the sessions safely, modelling the activities and the specific vocabulary. Throughout the unit, children should be encouraged to 'own the whole process'; therefore, it is strongly recommended that the adult does not draw on the children's work, instead modelling examples in their own (adult's) sketchbook.

You may wish to record the activities using a camera.

Natural connections

- Exploration of colours, lines, patterns, textures and shapes in nature
- Identifying plants and seasonal changes.

Health and wellbeing

- Physical activity
- Prolonging focus
- Emotional wellbeing
- Expressing feelings
- Problem-solving
- Learning new skills.

Word bank

Colour

- primary and secondary colours
- limited palette
- tone
- shade
- blending
- smudging

Texture, pattern

- rough
- smooth
- jagged
- symmetrical
- dabbing

Line, shape, form

- sketch
- outline
- illustrator
- form
- shades
- protruding

Composition

- composition
- placement
- spatial organisation
- aesthetically pleasing
- arrangement
- viewfinder

Summary overview

Progression	Curriculum content	Learning experiences/activities
Lesson 1	To use sketchbooks to record their observations and use them to review and revisit ideas. To improve their mastery of art and design techniques, including drawing with a range of materials.	The children learn about the primatologist Jane Goodall and about recording animals and plants through sketches. They investigate the techniques used in an illustrated book, and then record their own observations of the setting in their sketchbooks.
Lesson 2	To use sketchbooks to record their observations and use them to review and revisit ideas. To improve their mastery of art and design techniques, including drawing and painting with a range of materials.	The children discuss colours and identify different leaves. They investigate the colours and techniques used in an illustrated book about colours. They then collect observations of one colour, using different techniques to record the colour in their sketchbooks.
Lesson 3	To use sketchbooks to record their observations and use them to review and revisit ideas. To improve their mastery of art and design techniques, including drawing and painting with a range of materials.	The children discuss the colours, features and shapes of leaves. They investigate the colours and techniques used in an illustrated book about autumnal changes. They then draw trees in the setting using different techniques.
Lesson 4	To use sketchbooks to record their observations and use them to review and revisit ideas. To improve their mastery of art and design techniques, including drawing and painting with a range of materials.	The children explore different textures using natural objects. They investigate the textures and techniques used in an illustrated book about nature at night. They then use a new technique to record natural textures.
Lesson 5	To use sketchbooks to record their observations and use them to review and revisit ideas. To improve their mastery of art and design techniques, including drawing and painting with a range of materials.	The children learn how to use a viewfinder to focus on objects and compose their drawings. They investigate the composition and techniques used in a book featuring plant illustrations. They then use a viewfinder to compose their own drawings of plants.
Lesson 6	To use sketchbooks to record their observations and use them to review and revisit ideas. To improve their mastery of art and design techniques, including sculpture with a range of materials. To learn about great artists in history.	Children explore form using clay. They play the 'spotters' game, looking for unusual features. They observe examples of portraits by great artists, exploring how emotions change facial expressions. They investigate the 'form' of a face, before pressing clay into the bark of a tree and sculpting a face expressing a specific emotion. They may also draw their creation in their sketchbook, using pencil shading,

PREPARATION

Use a plant guide to check for harmful plants and berries in the outdoor area. At the start of the session, make the children aware of these by marking them in some way, e.g. by attaching a red ribbon as a warning not to use them in the session.

Resources

- An illustrated book about Jane Goodall, chimpanzees or another naturalist, such as *Me... Jane*, written and illustrated by Patrick McDonnell

- Sketchbooks or paper and clipboards

- Soft drawing pencils

- Soft coloured pencils, wax or oil pastels or crayons

- Pencil sharpeners

- Selection of non-fiction books or identification guides with illustrations of plants and animals (including minibeasts) found in the area

Previous learning

This progression reinforces and extends learning from Year 3 science (plants) and Year 3 reading comprehension.

CONSIDER

Health & Safety

Assess and evaluate hazards and risks in your setting. See the health and safety chapter.

LESSON OBJECTIVES

We are starting to use sketching techniques to collect information about nature.

National Curriculum Content

- To start to use sketchbooks to record observations and use them to review and revisit ideas.

- To begin to improve their mastery of art and design techniques, including drawing, with a range of materials.

ADULT ROLES

- Encourage the use of technical art vocabulary.

- Ask questions such as 'Can you see how... ?'

- Ensure that the plants being collected or observed are not hazardous.

WARM UP IDEAS

Explain that for the next six sessions, the children will be going to the outdoor learning area to do their art sessions. How does this make them feel? What will it be like?

Assess prior learning and understanding by briefly introducing (or revising) visual arts terminology, such as 'colour', 'pattern', 'texture', 'line', 'shape' and 'form'. What do they understand by these terms and can they give examples of each?

Introduce the life of Jane Goodall

Ask the children whether they have heard of Jane Goodall. Explain that Jane Goodall is a primatologist – someone who studies apes and monkeys. As a child, she was fascinated by animals and dreamt of being able to watch and write about animals. In her twenties, she started a project observing and studying the lives of chimpanzees in Tanzania. She made several ground-breaking discoveries, including that chimpanzees make and use tools.

As a child, she loved to draw animals and plants and make notes in a sketchbook, and this book tells her story. Explain that they will be making their own drawings and notes in their sketchbooks just like Jane Goodall, and this book will show them how to do this.

Nature sketches

Sharing the book (whole class)

Read the book to the class, introducing visual arts terminology (sketches, the illustrator's use of colour, how outlines are used, placement and composition on the page) and highlighting examples in the illustrations. What does the illustration do? What is the purpose of the illustrations?

What animals are in the book? Are we likely to find these in the outdoor learning area? Why not?

Challenge 1 (groups of four)

Identify different drawing techniques

On reaching the end of the book, explain that the children will be looking in detail at the illustrations.

Give the groups time to study the pages, encouraging them to identify the techniques used by the illustrator and how the illustrations have been presented on the page, such as a collection of subjects on one page, sketched, with some close-up or detailed illustrations, occasionally using colour, words to add description, etc. Discuss who the drawings are for, as well as whether they are effective and why.

Challenge 2 (whole class)

What lives in the outdoor area?

Groups feed back their discussion to the class.

Revise (or introduce) the term 'biodiversity', clarifying the meaning ('a variety of plant and animal life found in the world or in a particular habitat'). Why is biodiversity important?

Link to Year 3 science by remembering the requirements of plants for life and growth (air, light, water, nutrients from the soil and room to grow).

What animals and plants might they find in the outdoor learning area? This may link to previous studies conducted in the setting, such as plant and minibeast hunts.

How will they identify what it is that they have found?

Introduce and explain how to use the information books and/or identification sheets.

Challenge 3 (individual and small groups)

Draw and collect information like Jane Goodall

Model how to secure the sketchbook to the clipboard, draw an outline, draw detail and add words to describe a plant's colour, size or patterns.

Show how to take a rubbing of a leaf or of tree bark. This can be on a separate piece of paper, which can be stuck into the sketchbook.

Explain that the children will be exploring the area, making drawings in their sketchbooks of plants and animals that they find. They need to identify and add notes next to their sketch, just like Jane Goodall.

- They must decide where on the page their drawing will be, considering placement. Does it need to be in the middle of the page?

- They may decide to place their sketch or words in a box. What effect would this have on the page?

- In pairs or small groups, the children explore the area, identifying plants and recording their findings.

Encourage the children to explain what they have done in the session. What did the children find out about drawing techniques or plants and animals in the outdoor area? How did they create their sketches?

Back in the classroom

Visit Jane Goodall's site www.rootsnshoots.org.uk – an education programme for children to find out more about her work.

The children could review their sketches to revisit design ideas or to use them for science illustrations.

- What went well and why?
- What didn't go as well as expected?
- What could be changed?
- Who stood out and why?

PREPARATION

Use a plant guide to check for harmful plants and berries in the outdoor area. At the start of the session, make the children aware of these by marking them in some way, e.g. attaching a red ribbon as a warning not to use them in the session.

Resources

- An illustrated book about colour or which uses lots of colour, such as *Hailstones and Halibut Bones* by Mary O'Neill

- Selection of leaves and plants from the area

- Leaf and plant identification guide from www. woodlandtrust.org. uk/naturedetectives/ activities/2015/09/leaf-id

- Clipboards, paper, sketchbooks and drawing pencils

- Coloured crayons, pastels (a variety of shades of each colour) or watercolour paint boxes and fine-tipped brushes

Previous learning

This session reinforces learning from Year 3 science (plants) and Year 3 reading comprehension.

CONSIDER

Health & Safety

Assess and evaluate hazards and risks in your setting. See the health and safety chapter.

LESSON OBJECTIVES

We are exploring ways of recording colours found in nature.

National Curriculum Content

- To start to use sketchbooks to record observations and use them to review and revisit ideas.

- To begin to improve their mastery of art and design techniques, including drawing and painting, with a range of materials.

ADULT ROLES

- Encourage careful observation.

- Ask questions such as 'Can you see how... ?' rather than give directions.

- Encourage use of art vocabulary.

WARM UP IDEAS

Explain that this session, the children will be exploring and studying colour and recording it in their sketchbooks.

Revise visual arts terminology relating to colour. For example:

- What are the primary colours and what makes them primary colours?

- What happens when you mix two primary colours?

- What secondary colours can you name?

This provides an opportunity to revise colour-mixing (reinforcing Key Stage 1 art).

Introduce the book

Explain what the book is about and how it features colour. Preview the book by showing that colours are illustrated on each page and described in words. Discuss how colours can link with emotions. Have they linked colours and emotions before? If we are feeling 'blue', what does this mean?

Explain that they will be making their own drawings and notes about colours they find in the area in their sketchbooks, as in Progression 1. They can also use words to describe the colours they find (although this can be done as a follow-up back in the classroom if preferred).

What coloured leaves and plants are they likely to find in the setting?

Show the children a selection of leaves and plants from the area or go on a one-minute plant hunt.

- Show the children the leaf/plant identification guide.

- Point out key features of the plants, such as colours or jagged edges.

- Link to Year 3 science by identifying the structure and function of leaves.

- Can they match and identify their findings using an identification guide?

Recording natural colours

Share the book

Either read the whole book or select a few of the pages which use colours found in the outdoor learning area, highlighting examples in the illustrations.

Look at how objects are arranged together on a page (placement and composition).
Do they like this idea? Why? Is it effective?

Consider the illustrator's use of colour, introducing and explaining the terms 'shades' and 'tones', e.g. their use of primary or secondary colours, how outlines using similar colours are used, placement on the page.

Consider how words in the book are used to describe colour. Reinforce the technical vocabulary 'tones' and 'shades', and use the phrase 'limited palette' to describe only using a small range of colours.

- PSHE links: Explore the description and expression of feelings using colour. Do they have 'hot' or 'red' feelings? Would this be a good way to tell someone how you are feeling?

- Science links: What plants, objects and subjects are described in the book? Ask whether we are likely to find these in the outdoor learning area. Point out how light is reflected from surfaces, and how shadows might be represented in a painting.

Challenge 1 (in pairs or groups of four)

Identify different drawing techniques

Allow groups time to study the pages, encouraging them to identify and ask questions about the techniques used and how these have been presented on the page, i.e. a collection of subjects on one page, drawn or coloured using watercolour and limited palette, discussing and hypothesising in their group. What techniques they have identified? How effective are the techniques and why? What purpose do the illustrations serve? Who are the illustrations for?

Challenge 2 (individuals in pairs or groups of four)

Draw plants and record colours

Decide on one colour to 'collect' and draw an outline of one item from observation, emphasising 'look, draw, look again, draw' – reinforcing observation, studying the object for details and adding these, writing words to describe the colour, size or patterns, and thinking about the composition using careful placement on the page.

Who might this artwork be for and how might the artwork look different for different purposes?

- Show how to blend pencil, crayon or pastel colours by overlaying or 'smudging', using a limited palette (of the chosen colour).

- Show how to use the watercolour boxes, adding a small amount of colour to the wet tip of the brush and mixing in the lid of the box, demonstrating how to make it lighter (more water or adding a touch of white) or darker (more pigment or adding a touch of black).

- In pairs or small groups, the children explore the area, recording their plant and colour findings in their sketchbooks, while considering placement and leaving space for captions.

Ask the children what they have discovered. Can they identify the plants they have drawn?

Back in the classroom

- Write your own colour poem

- Look at your sketches – would you draw them differently next time?

- What went well and why?
- What didn't go as well as expected?
- What could be changed?
- Who stood out and why?

PREPARATION

Use a plant guide to check for harmful plants and berries in the outdoor area.

Collect large leaves, such as sycamore or dock leaves, and break them into pieces, placing each leaf jigsaw in a separate envelope or on separate tree stumps.

Resources

- An illustrated book about autumnal changes, such as *Fletcher and the Falling Leaves* by Julia Rawlinson, illustrated by Tiphanie Beeke

- Selection of fallen leaves from the area

- Leaf jigsaw pieces

- Leaf identification guide: www.woodlandtrust. org.uk/naturedetectives/ activities/2015/09/leaf-id

- Magnifying glasses

- Clipboards, sketchbooks, paper and pencils

- Coloured crayons or pastels (a variety of shades of each colour)

- Optional: watercolour boxes and thin-tipped brushes

- Optional: mud and natural pigments

Previous learning

Activities in this progression reinforce Progression 1 and learning from Year 3 science (plants) and Year 3 reading comprehension.

CONSIDER

Health & Safety

Assess and evaluate hazards and risks in your setting. See the health and safety chapter.

LESSON OBJECTIVES

We are learning how to record colours and shapes from nature.

National Curriculum Content

- To start to use sketchbooks to record observations and use them to review and revisit ideas.

- To begin to improve mastery of art and design techniques, including drawing and painting, with a range of materials.

ADULT ROLES

- Encouraging careful observation.

- Asking questions such as 'Can you see how... ?'

- Encouraging use of art vocabulary.

WARM UP IDEAS

Explain that this session, the children will be exploring and studying the colour and shape of leaves and trees, continuing to use their sketchbook to record their work.

What leaves and plants are they likely to find in the setting? (whole class and in pairs)

Show the children a selection of leaves and plants from the area or go on a one-minute plant hunt.

Independently or using the leaf identification guide, can they identify the leaves?

With a talking partner and using magnifying glasses, share details of the leaves, including the colours and patterns that they can see. Ask the children to use visual arts terminology relating to 'colour', such as primary or secondary colours, tones, shades or limited palette.

- Are the leaves all one colour or can they see evidence of other colours, shades or tones?

- Can they describe these colours and patterns to one another?

Link to Year 3 science by discussing seasonal changes, such as how or why leaves change colour or fall from the trees.

Leaf jigsaw activity (groups of four)

In groups, the challenge is to put a torn leaf back together.

- What is the type of leaf that they have as their jigsaw? How do they know?

- What are the identifying features? What shape is it and how can it be described?

- What colours (shades and tones) can they see in their leaf?

- Use a magnifying glass to really observe the colours and lines on the leaf.

Recording natural shapes

Share the book

Explain that children will be making their own drawings in their sketchbooks, recording studies of leaves and trees from the area, inspired by the book you will read together.

Read the book to the group, discussing the changes that happen in autumn.

Highlight examples of the bold colours in the illustrations, looking at the illustrator's use of autumnal colours and textures.

Challenge 1 (in pairs and groups of four)

Identify examples of different art techniques

Allow the children time to study the pages from the book, encouraging them to identify the techniques used and discuss these with others.

- Are primary or secondary colours used? What colours could have been used to create the secondary colours?

- Are outlines used? What about placement on the page?

- What medium do they think was used, e.g. watercolour, pastels, wax crayons?

- Do the colours change during the story? Why is this?

- Are the illustrations very detailed or quite rough?

- Focus on the trees: how are they painted?

Ask the children what techniques they have identified. How effective are the techniques and why?

Challenge 2 (in pairs)

Identify leaves from the area

Ask the children to explain to a partner what happens to tree leaves in the autumn. Share ideas with the group (Key Stage 1 science and geography links).

A great explanation can be found at: www.woodlandtrust.org.uk/blog/2018/10/why-autumn-leaves-change-colour.

How do the trees in the setting change? Have they changed since the children's last visit? Why is this?

Challenge 3 (whole class, in pairs or groups of four)

Draw trees and record colours and shapes

Show how to use bold strokes of oil pastel colours to draw a tree from the area, varying the colours and adding texture using dabbing, colours and blotting, thinking about the composition and using careful placement.

Emphasise the 'spaces' between the branches so that the sky shines through.

Add leaves using simple shapes, choosing colour and angle of leaf carefully.

- Optional: Revise how to use the watercolour boxes, adding a small amount of colour to the wet tip of the brush and mixing in the lid of the box, demonstrating how to make it lighter (more water or adding a touch of white) or darker (more pigment or adding a touch of black). Why can't it be too wet?

In pairs or small groups, the children explore the area, drawing trees and leaves from the area using bold pastel colours in their sketchbooks (or on separate paper if preferred).

They must decide where on the page their drawing will be, considering placement, e.g. does it need to be in the middle of the page?

- Optional: Children can make their own brown paints and pigments from the outdoor learning area, e.g. by using mud or soil. They can reflect on the advantages and disadvantages of this.

PLENARY

Encourage the children to explain, in groups and as a whole class, what they have been doing in the session and state what they have learned about colour, shape and their favourite art technique.

EVALUATION/FOLLOW ON

- What went well and why?

- What didn't go as well as expected?

- What could be changed?

- Who stood out and why?

PREPARATION

Check the area for hazardous plants and berries and make the children aware of them.

Prepare a wax resist drawing beforehand, applying ink over the top and allowing it to thoroughly dry. See the following for a similar technique using paint: www.youtube.com/watch?v=RowwC13rBRs. You may wish to practise this once or twice to perfect the polishing technique.

Resources

• An illustrated book about nighttime in nature or nocturnal animals, such as *Dark Emperor and Other Poems of the Night* by Joyce Sidman, illustrated by Rick Allen

• Soft bag that can be sealed at the top

• Selection of textured natural objects such as bark, feather, pinecones, leaves, etc.

• Clipboards, sketchbooks, paper and pencils

• Selection of brightly coloured wax crayons

• Black Indian ink (or black watercolour paint), cotton wool balls and gloves

• Soft cloth

Previous learning

Activities in this progression reinforce learning from Year 3 science (plants) and Year 3 reading comprehension.

CONSIDER

Health & Safety

Assess and evaluate hazards and risks in your setting. See the health and safety chapter.

LESSON OBJECTIVES

We are finding textures in the outdoor area and exploring how these can be recorded using wax resist technique.

National Curriculum Content

• To start to use sketchbooks to record observations and use them to review and revisit ideas.

• To begin to improve mastery of art and design techniques, including drawing and painting, with a range of materials.

ADULT ROLES

• Asking questions such as 'Can you see how... ?'

• Encourage use of art vocabulary.

• Modelling the activity, checking for bold wax application and applying the ink (wearing gloves).

WARM UP IDEAS

Discussing changes and textures (whole class and in pairs)

Look around the area and ask whether children notice any changes. What are the changes and why have they occurred? Can they hypothesise why this may have happened?

Children share sketchbooks with a partner, reviewing and revisiting ideas from previous sessions and discussing the colours, shapes and patterns they have found in the learning area. Encourage the children to use visual arts terminology relating to the artwork they have produced (see word bank).

Ask the children to explain what a 'texture' is. What examples can be found in the learning area? When they did bark rubbings in Progression 1, they were recording texture.

Feely bag activity (whole class)

Secretly place a textured item into the bag (see resources).

• Choose one child to place their hand in the bag and describe what they can feel, without naming the object.

• Can the other children guess what it is from the description?

• Remove the item from the bag.

• What can they see and what does it look like?

Explain that 'texture' is the way things feel or the way things look like they might feel.

Repeat the activity with other children, providing a variety of items for the children to touch and feel, such as tree bark, pinecones or hairy leaves.

What adjectives can they use to describe their object?

Link to science by stating the function of the object, e.g. reproduction, nutrition, support.

MAIN ACTIVITIES

Nature's textures and wax resist

Share the book

Explain that children will be recording studies of textures in leaves and trees from the area in their sketchbooks.

The book describes what happens when we are asleep and all is dark and still. But what does it tell us about nocturnal wildlife?

- Would we find the same creatures at night in the learning area?

- Does the learning area provide the same habitats?
- What similarities are there?

Challenge 1 (in pairs or groups of four)

Identify examples of different art techniques

Allow the children time to study and discuss the pages from the book, encouraging them to identify techniques such as short strokes and use of lines to create texture.

- What colours have been used?
- Do the illustrations have much detail, or not?
- Focus on trees, e.g. how is the bark texture shown?

Ask the children what techniques they have identified. How effective are the techniques and why?

Challenge 2 (whole class, in pairs or groups)

Draw trees and plants, recording textures

Show how to use bold application of wax crayons or wax pastels to represent tree bark, leaf textures or spider's webs, using short but firm dabbing strokes and leaving spaces between textures so the paper is visible.

- Use the lightest colours, but not black. Most of the page needs to be waxed, so consider 'scale' and placement. Explain that dark colours will be added during the next step.

- Wearing gloves, apply black Indian ink to the surface of the waxed drawing, using cotton wool.

- Show how the thickly applied wax resists the ink, but some of the picture will appear black. Emphasise that the wax needs to be thickly applied for the technique to be most effective.

- Using the prepared wax resist picture show how, when dry and gently polished, the wax shines through the ink, leaving the non-waxed areas black. Or scratch the black away with a sharp stick to reveal the wax underneath and create 'spiky' textures.

Groups explore the area, studying tree and leaf textures using bold wax colours as demonstrated, in their sketchbooks.

It is recommended that an adult applies the ink, checking that the drawing has a good, bold covering of wax beforehand (take a photo if unsure so the work is recorded). Leave the picture to dry overnight.

PLENARY

Encourage the children to explain their artwork techniques and state what they have learned. Reflect on the amount of detail they hope to see in their textured pictures.

Back in the classroom

The children either polish the drawing using a soft cloth or use a sharp stick to reveal the hidden image. Use Styrofoam printing to create printed texture pictures and compare them with the wax resist method.

EVALUATION/FOLLOW ON

- What went well and why?
- What didn't go as well as expected?
- What could be changed?
- Who stood out and why?

PREPARATION

Check the area for harmful plants and make the children aware of them.

Make or source the viewfinders. These can be sourced from picture framers (as inner mount frames are often discarded) or see www.liveabout.com/viewfinder-art-2578087.

Resources

- An illustrated book featuring plant illustrations and about gardening or natural areas, such as *The Little Gardener* by Emily Hughes

- Selection of fallen leaves from the area

- Plant identification guide: www.woodlandtrust.org.uk/naturedetectives/activities/2015/09/leaf-id

- Magnifying glasses

- Viewfinders

- Clipboards, sketchbooks, paper and pencils

- Coloured crayons or pastels

- Optional: watercolour boxes and thin-tipped brushes

Previous learning

Activities in this progression reinforce learning from Year 3 science (plants) and Year 3 reading comprehension.

CONSIDER

Health & Safety

Assess and evaluate hazards and risks in your setting. See the health and safety chapter.

LESSON OBJECTIVES

We are learning to use a viewfinder to explore composition when drawing plants.

National Curriculum Content

- To start to use sketchbooks to record observations and use them to review and revisit ideas.

- To begin to improve mastery of art and design techniques, including drawing and painting, with a range of materials.

ADULT ROLES

- Model the activity, encouraging careful observation.

- Ask questions such as 'Can you see how... ?'

- Look for and praise examples where shape and line work well, pointing out improvements they have made.

- Encourage use of art vocabulary.

WARM UP IDEAS

Ask the children to talk to a partner about any changes they have noticed in the outdoor learning area since the previous session. Can they explain why this is so?

Explain that today the children will be exploring and studying the colour and shape of leaves and plants, continuing to use their sketchbook to record their work. But this time they will have the option of adding a figure, perhaps representing themselves or a friend within the picture.

What leaves and plants are they likely to find in the setting?

Show the children a selection of leaves and plants from the area or go on a one-minute plant hunt.

Independently or using the leaf identification guide, can they identify the leaves?

With a talking partner and using magnifying glasses, share details of the leaves, including the colours and patterns that they can see.

Introduce the viewfinder to focus on particular parts or plants

Show how it can be used like a camera viewfinder to zoom in and out or 'crop' the image (computing links).

Show how to choose 'portrait' or 'landscape' format and how it can be moved up, down, to the side or at an angle to 'compose' the picture.

Use the viewfinder to zoom in and out, using the leaves and plants in the area as a focus.

MAIN ACTIVITIES

Plant focus

Share the book

Explain that they will be making their own drawings in their sketchbooks, recording studies of textures in leaves and plants from the area and adding a figure within their composition. Explain that you have chosen a book to demonstrate what it could look like and how it could be done.

Read the book to the class.

- Could the story be told without the words, simply using the illustrations?

- Who do they think the book is aimed at? Why is this?

- Make links with the character and how they feel about their own growing areas (if appropriate) – do they ever feel that their garden is out of control and the weeds are taking over? How do they feel when the garden flourishes?

Challenge 1
(whole class and in pairs or groups of four)

Identify examples of different art techniques

Studying the illustrations, highlight the techniques the illustrator has used. How could they be copied? Do the plants in the book look as if they have been individually drawn and placed on the page? In the school's outdoor space, are plants spaced out or arranged in groups? Why?

How is the beauty of the plants and flowers created, e.g. placement and dominance on the page, amount of detail, the bright colours (tones and shades) and lines?

Using a real flower or plant, demonstrate the use of the viewfinder to 'zoom in' so that the flower fills the frame.

Allow the children time to study and discuss the pages from the book, encouraging them to identify the techniques that may have been used to create the images.

- What medium and colours have been used?

- Are the illustrations very detailed or sketchy?

- Focus on the leaves and flowers, e.g. how is the leaf structure or the detail highlighted or emphasised?

- How are the plants arranged on the page?

- Optional: How is the figure drawn and how is it placed on the page?

Ask the children what techniques they have identified. How effective are the techniques and why?

Challenge 2
(whole class and in pairs or groups of four)

Draw trees and plants, recording textures, lines and details

Show how to use the viewfinder to choose a subject to focus on. Draw an outline of a plant from the area, adding fill colours and using careful placement. Revise how to use the watercolour boxes (see previous progressions), showing how to apply the paint and infill the outlines.

- Optional: Show how to add a figure in the picture.

In pairs or small groups, the children explore the area looking for plants and leaves, practising 'framing their work' using the viewfinder to compose their subject. They decide where on the page their drawing will be, considering placement before drawing it in their sketchbooks and adding colour. They can include multiple plants on their page.

- Optional: Add a figure or person to their drawing.

PLENARY

Encourage the children to explain what they have been doing and state what they have noticed about the improvements in their work. Why is this? Share and review their work with a trusted partner or in small groups. Compare their drawings, emphasising technical elements and whether they capture the 'essence' of the plants they have drawn.

EVALUATION/FOLLOW ON

- What went well and why?

- What didn't go as well as expected?

- What could be changed?

- Who stood out and why?

PREPARATION

Use a plant guide to check for harmful plants and berries in the outdoor area.

Source images of famous portrait artwork that show strong facial expressions, such as those by Edvard Munch, Van Gogh, Matisse, etc.

Resources

- Examples of portrait paintings by great artists
- Sketchbooks, paper and pencils
- Clay
- Water

Previous learning

This unit links to Year 3 science.

CONSIDER

Health & Safety

Assess and evaluate hazards and risks in your setting. See the health and safety chapter.

LESSON OBJECTIVES

We are exploring shape and form by sketching and making clay tree spirits.

National Curriculum Content

- To start to use sketchbooks to record their observations and use them to review and revisit ideas.
- To improve their mastery of art and design techniques, including sculpture with a range of materials.
- To learn about great artists in history.

ADULT ROLES

- Encourage the children to consider form and shape their clay before adding bits.

WARM UP IDEAS

Revise the previous progressions, using the art-specific vocabulary to explore colour, line, pattern and texture. Explain that in this session the children will be exploring and studying shape and form, using their sketchbook to record their work. Can they remember what the words 'shape' and 'form' (representation of a 3D shape) mean?

Look around the outdoor area, observing changes, and discuss why these may have occurred.

Is there anything that they notice now that they haven't noticed before? Why is that? Can they think of imaginative explanations?

Spotters (in pairs)

1. Children walk around the outdoor learning area, looking for changes since their last visit.
2. They carefully explore until something catches their attention. This could be something big or small, a flash of colour, a small detail or part of something bigger, the shape of a group of plants or trees, a new smell, a drip of sap, a face-like shape in the textured bark of a tree, etc.
3. The spotter says: 'I can see something!'
4. Partner asks: 'What can you see?'
5. Spotter describes, in great detail, what they are looking at, giving the context too, e.g. 'I can see two eyes staring at me from deep inside a tree. They glistened and moved. I think it is something that lives in the tree.' Encourage the use of art vocabulary to describe details such as textures, pattern, shape, colour tones and shades.
6. Partner asks: 'How does it make you feel?'
7. Spotter explains how it made them feel when they spotted it. What has caused their reaction to seeing it? How it is making them feel now? They should use their imagination to extend their responses.
8. Continue to explore the area, taking it in turns to spot things that catch their eye, describing it in detail and explaining how it makes them feel.

MAIN ACTIVITIES

Tree spirit forms

Explore representation of shape and form in the work of great artists (whole class, in pairs)

When children were doing the 'spotters' activity, did they spot any textures or patterns on tree bark or see strange tree faces or creatures? Explain that they are going to create their own tree faces using clay. Have they done this before? Have they used clay before? Link to Year 3 science (rocks) by asking whether they knew that clay comes from rock (it is a natural material made up of tiny particles of rock; when added to water, it goes soft, like mud).

1. Ask the children to model different facial expressions to a partner, e.g. angry, sad, happy, thoughtful, fearful, etc.
2. Show the examples of portraits by great artists, studying the emotions that are expressed and how this might have been achieved, such as mouth shape, positions of the eyes, eyebrows, etc.
3. Ask the children to model the expressions again, but this time feeling their own faces to feel how the expressions change the face.
4. Feel how the nose is part of the face and blends with the cheeks and how the cheeks travel around to the ears.
5. Feel the mouth position in relation to the nose and chin. Watch and observe a partner making the faces again, focusing on these parts of the face.
6. Place both hands over the face to feel how it fits into the curved palms, but with the nose protruding.

Challenge 1 (whole class, individual or in pairs)

Explore techniques used to form clay into a face

Demonstrate how to mould the clay into the shape of a head and press this into the bark of a tree.

1. Clarifying the word 'form' to show how the face is being shaped, rather than drawing details on the surface, show how to squeeze and press the clay to form a projecting nose, forehead, chin, cheeks and other features, depicting a specific emotion.
2. Show how to use water to blend and smooth the clay and get rid of cracks.
3. Ask the children what other details should be added, such as textures of hair, lines on the face, etc. Why add these? What effect could they have?
4. Ask how these could be achieved, modelling the children's examples and showing how to create lines and patterns by drawing with sticks or imprinting textured natural objects into the clay.

5. Show how to add natural objects to the face to add features, by pushing items into the clay, such as leaves, moss or lichen for hair or beards, acorns and beech-nuts for eyes, etc.

In pairs or working individually and independently, the children create their own tree spirits' faces out of clay, expressing an emotion and considering form.

They add detail using natural materials, considering form, texture and line, and record the faces using a camera, demonstrating how to choose an interesting viewing angle.

Optional extension

Can they draw the clay face in their sketchbooks?

They should start by drawing the 'outline' and some features of the face in the sketchbook.

Show how to identify light and shade and use the pencil to colour the shaded parts, linking to science (light).

PLENARY

Encourage the children to explain what they have been doing in the session and state what they have learned about portraits and form. Share their tree faces, pointing out the formed features and how they were achieved. Consider and discuss what feelings the faces express and how this has been achieved. How effective is it?

Review the unit. What was their favourite part? Use the sketchbooks to review and revisit ideas. If time allows, the children can choose to repeat their favourite activity or an activity in which they want to make further improvements, exploring in more depth or with a different approach.

EVALUATION/FOLLOW ON

- What went well and why?
- What didn't go as well as expected?
- What could be changed?
- Who stood out and why?

Design and Technology

Based on the Key Stage 2 design and technology (DT) attainment targets identified in the 2014 National Curriculum for England, in this unit children design a fantasy world in the outdoor learning area, for use by the whole school to stimulate imaginative and creative writing, through an exploration of structures and materials. Technical knowledge and skills from Key Stage 1 DT are reinforced and extended through a variety of creative and practical activities in the context of the outdoors, by learning a variety of component-joining and tool-use techniques by drawing plans and diagrams and using and applying learning linked to geometry, calculation, estimation and measures from the Year 3 numeracy objectives.

To support inclusive practice or to extend learning, the space, task, equipment and people (STEP) approach can be adopted throughout this unit. By changing the space, task, equipment or people, the activity can be made more challenging or easier to understand, enabling all pupils to take part in the activity, as explained in the assessment chapter. In the context of design technology, this could mean providing a well-defined learning space, positioning pupils away from potential distractions, considering whether the task needs to be simplified by breaking it down into component parts or extended by making it more challenging, using smaller or lightweight tools such as palm drills or small power tools in order to make the task more accessible, working independently on a specified task, or working in small groups, with a buddy or with an adult as appropriate.

The role of the adult is to lead the sessions safely whilst providing direct support and reassurance as appropriate.

You may wish to record the activities using a camera.

Natural connections

- Enhanced awareness of their local environment
- Exploration and evaluation of man-made structures
- Awareness of humans' impact on the environment.

Health and wellbeing

- Physical activity
- Being creative and evaluative
- Designing with purpose
- Safety management
- Appreciating aesthetics
- Protecting and enhancing environments.

Word bank

Design

- structure
- stable
- function
- purpose
- crossbar
- cross brace, ladder
- decorative elements
- safety

Materials

- strength
- strengthening
- attractive
- flexible
- rigid
- peg
- dowel

Skills

- technical knowledge
- secateurs
- loppers
- saw
- diagonal/square /floor/ ladder lashing
- half-lap joint

Summary overview

Progression	Curriculum content	Learning experiences/activities
Lesson 1	Throughout this unit, children will: Use research and develop design criteria to inform design of innovative, functional and appealing products, fit for purpose and aimed at specific individuals or groups.	Children explore the definitions of 'fantasy setting' and 'structures'. They examine existing crossbar structures and cross bracing in the setting, investigating their purpose, functional properties, material and construction, promoting understanding of how to join, strengthen, stiffen and reinforce more complex structures. They use square lashing (or other options if suitable) to make their own cross. They add functional and decorative features. They draw and label their structure and evaluate their designs.
Lesson 2	Generate, develop, model and communicate ideas through discussion and sketches. Select from and use a wider range of tools and equipment to perform practical tasks accurately.	Children explore existing frame structures and products in the setting, investigating their purpose, functional properties, material and construction, promoting understanding of how to join, strengthen, stiffen and reinforce more complex structures. They use joining techniques (square lashing with the option to use half-lap joints or notches in an adult-led group) to make their own frame. They decide on its purpose, adding functional and decorative features, draw and label their structure, and evaluate their designs.
Lesson 3	Select from and use a wider range of materials and components, including construction materials, according to their functional properties and aesthetic qualities. Investigate and analyse a range of existing products.	Children explore existing decking, fencing or bridge-type structures and products in the setting, investigating their purpose, functional properties, material and construction, promoting understanding of how to join, strengthen, stiffen and reinforce more complex structures. They use joining techniques (with the option to use ladder lashing) to make their own parallel structure. They decide on its purpose, adding functional and decorative features. They draw and label their structure and evaluate their designs.
Lesson 4	Evaluate their ideas and products against their own design criteria and consider the views of others to improve their work. Apply their understanding of how to strengthen, stiffen and reinforce more complex structures.	Children explore existing step and ladder structures and products in the setting, investigating their purpose, functional properties, material and construction, promoting understanding of how to join, strengthen, stiffen and reinforce more complex structures. They use joining techniques, including ladder lashing, to make their own step- and ladder-based structure. They decide on its purpose, adding functional and decorative features. They draw and label their structure and evaluate their designs.
Lesson 5		Children apply the technical knowledge and skills they have gained through previous progressions in small groups to choose a setting and design for a fantasy world in the outdoor learning area, using ideas from the prototypes they have produced in Progressions 1–4, and original ideas based on research carried out in school and at home. They decide on the location and what can be built there. They draw and label structure designs in situ, considering the materials and tools available. They decide on an order of work and the roles and work outcomes for each team member. They share their ideas with the rest of the group, considering any views and making amendments as necessary.
Lesson 6		Children apply the technical knowledge and skills they have gained through Progressions 1–4 to create a fantasy world in the outdoor learning area. They work in their groups to complete the design brief of 'fantasy'. They evaluate their own products and those of other groups.

PREPARATION

Source the location of suitable crossbar and cross brace structures to explore and evaluate, such as crosses in window panes, on doors, fences or railings, on shelving, electricity pylons, roof trusses, playground equipment, swing frames, etc.

Source images of crossbars and cross braces to show the children during the introduction.

Resources

- Images of crossbars and cross braces in structures
- Variety of sticks
- String or cord
- Optional: scrap material for decoration
- Paper, pencils and clipboards
- Scissors
- Rulers
- Optional tool use: drill, secateurs, saw, knives, rasps or peelers, safety gloves

CONSIDER

Health & Safety

Assess and evaluate hazards and risks in your setting. See the health and safety chapter.

LESSON OBJECTIVES

We are exploring crossbars and braces in structures and how they are used to strengthen and stabilise.

National Curriculum Content

- Investigate and analyse a range of existing products.
- Use research and develop design criteria to inform the design of innovative, functional, appealing products that are fit for purpose and aimed at particular individuals or groups.

ADULT ROLES

- Support the whole task by encouraging careful observation.
- Ask questions about what the children can see.
- Support with new skills but encourage the children to develop independence and help one another.

WARM UP IDEAS

Introduce the purpose of the next six sessions: the children will be investigating, designing and making fantasy world structures such as mini buildings, bridges, steps, doors and windows leading to fantasy worlds for use by the whole school for imaginative storytelling in the outdoor learning area.

Clarify the meaning of the word 'fantasy' by asking the children to provide examples of fantasy worlds that they know about or have experienced in books, such as *The Magic Far Away Tree*, *Alice in Wonderland* or *Through the Looking Glass* or *The Chronicles of Narnia*, films or computer games.

Clarify the word 'structure'. What type of structures might they find in a fantasy world and what do they look like? What previous experiences of making structures do they have?

Explain that they will be identifying specific 'functional elements' of structures to help them with their designs, and this week the focus will be on crossbars and cross braces, some of which are used for strengthening.

Give examples (see preparation) before asking the children to investigate the setting looking for existing crossbar and cross brace structures and sketching them, noting details of their design. Ask the children to investigate their purpose, functional properties, material and construction, promoting understanding of how to join, strengthen, stiffen and reinforce more complex structures.

MAIN ACTIVITIES

Crossbars and braces

Challenge 1 (whole class)

Modelling how to join two or more sticks in a cross, using lashing and drilling

Children observe and practise joining techniques, exploring how materials can be strengthened or made more stable. Show how working with a partner, who holds the sticks in place, may make this process easier.

1. Model how to join two sticks in a cross using square lashing. What makes it strong?

2. Optional: Model how to drill a hole in one stick and feed another stick (the correct width) through the hole to create a cross. This could form an introduction to peg or dowel joints. How can it be made stable and secure, e.g. by using and inserting a tapered stick?

3. Optional: If children are already familiar and confident with square lashing, then diagonal lashing can be introduced to extend technical knowledge.

4. Optional (not to be done by the children): Show how a simple half-lap joint is used to strengthen a joint. Remove a chunk from halfway along both of the sticks to be joined in the cross. The chunks should be as wide as the sticks and extend halfway into their girth. The sticks then fit into each other to make the cross.

Now the cross has been made, what could it be? What additional detail would need to be added to make it functional or appealing to match the brief of 'fantasy'? Take suggestions such as:

*   A fantasy stick figure – add a face, clothing made from scrap material and accessories.

*   A fantasy sword with special powers – wind string or wool around the 'handle' to create a grip.

*   A sail mast for a fantasy raft or boat – add the sail using leaves or material.

*   A fantasy flying object or plane – add the details by removing bark or with permanent markers and shape the wings.

*   A fantasy kite frame – add fabric to make a kite.

Optional tool use: Wearing safety gloves, model how to use secateurs and saws to cut to length or how to use knives, rasps or peelers to remove bark or marker pens to create other decorative details. Follow the tool safety principles in the health and safety chapter.

Introduce creating a 'design drawing', explaining that this would be used to show other people how to build their product, especially if it included measurements and quantities, by drawing the product from different angles, labelling functional properties and decorative features and identifying component materials.

Challenge 2 (individual or pairs)

Join two sticks to create a cross

The children source their own materials (sticks from the ground, tools and/or string) to create their own crossed-sticks products using the skills demonstrated or their own method, with adult-led groups where appropriate. They add detail to make it functional or appealing, to match the 'fantasy' brief.

When they have finished making, they draw their products from different angles and add annotations to evaluate the product. You may wish to model this process.

PLENARY

Encourage the children to explain what they have been doing in the session and state what they have found out.

Back in the classroom

Suggest that the children make a collection of pictures of fantasy worlds from the internet as research for their future designs, in preparation for the next progression.

EVALUATION/FOLLOW ON

*   What went well and why?
*   What didn't go as well as expected?
*   What could be changed?

PREPARATION

Source the location of suitable frame-based structures (some with cross bracing) to evaluate, e.g. window fastenings, football posts, playground equipment, doors, shelving, bike shelters, picture frames, etc.

Source images of the same to show during the warm up.

Resources

- Images of frame-based structures
- Variety of sticks
- String or cord
- Paper, pencils and clipboards
- Scissors
- Rulers
- Optional tool use: drill, secateurs, saw, knives, rasps or peelers, safety gloves
- Optional: PVA or wood glue, dowels, mirror

Previous learning

Remind the children of the purpose of the Design and Technology progressions: that they will be exploring, designing and building 'structures' to make a fantasy world or entrances to fantasy worlds in the outdoor learning area.

CONSIDER

Health & Safety

Assess and evaluate hazards and risks in your setting. See the health and safety chapter.

LESSON OBJECTIVES

We are exploring the functional features of frame-based structures and how they are joined and made strong.

National Curriculum Content

- Investigate and analyse a range of existing products.
- Select from and use a wider range of tools and equipment to perform practical tasks (for example, cutting, shaping, joining and finishing) accurately.
- Apply their understanding of how to strengthen, stiffen and reinforce more complex structures.

ADULT ROLES

- Support the whole task by encouraging careful observation.
- Ask questions about what the children can see.
- Support with new skills (including tool use) but encourage the children to develop independence, helping one another, cooperating and demonstrating safe practice.

WARM UP IDEAS

Ask the children to share their research and ideas following the previous session, including any illustrations of fantasy worlds for future designs, discussing how these might be applied to the outdoor learning area.

Inspect the outdoor learning area for suitable sites or settings for the fantasy structures. What are the criteria, taking into consideration the children's ideas and research, e.g. in a shaded area, close to interesting features such as mossy, stony or rocky areas, etc.?

Remind the children that each week they will be looking for specific functional properties of structures to help them with their designs. This week the focus is on frames. They will be continuing to look at the role of cross and diagonal braces, which are used for strengthening.

Give some examples before asking the children to explore the setting buildings, playground equipment and surroundings, looking for existing frame-based structures and how cross or diagonal bracing has been used to strengthen and stabilise these products.

Ask the children to investigate their purpose, functional properties, material and construction, looking at joints etc., promoting understanding of how to join, strengthen, stiffen and reinforce more complex structures.

MAIN ACTIVITIES

Frames

This activity can be adult-directed whole-class or group work with opportunities for individual experimentation.

The class could be divided in half, with groups working with adults to explore joining techniques whilst the other half explores the setting for possible placements, researches fantasy world structures and designs their own, before swapping. The same is true of the following four progressions.

Challenge 1 (whole class)

Revise how to join four sticks to form a rectangular frame

Observe and practise joining techniques, exploring how materials can be strengthened or made more stable. Using a partner to hold the sticks may help.

1. Model how to join the four sticks using square lashing. What makes it strong?
2. Optional: Model how to join the four sticks using drilling and pegging to make a dowel joint.
3. Optional: Show how simple half-lap joints at the ends of the sticks (see Progression 1) or a notch can also be used to help stabilise the joint. This is for demonstration purposes only and not recommended for the children at this age.

Now that the frame has been made, what could make it more stable and enable it to keep its shape?

Show how to attach diagonal bracing to the corners using lashing.

Optional: do this by drilling diagonal holes through the frame corner, inserting dowels and securing them with glue.

- How else could the product be strengthened?
- Does it have to be 'square' or have right angles?
- Would 'wonky' match the brief of 'fantasy'?
- Would it compromise strength and stability?

What could the frame be used for? What additional detail would need to be added to make it functional or appealing to match the brief of 'fantasy'? Take suggestions such as:

- A fantasy picture frame – decorate the frame and make a fantasy picture using found objects from the outdoor area to go in it.

- A mirror frame – to reflect the fantasy world inhabitants; decorate the frame and place it on a mirror or over still water.
- A door or window to the fantasy world – decorate the frame and add window crossbars or make and shape a doorframe, adding accessories such as a handle, letterbox, name-plate or keyhole.
- Challenge: Create a stilt framework structure from multiple frames, to raise a 'house' on stilts (the house could be made next week).

Optional tool use: Wearing safety gloves, model how to use knives, rasps or peelers to remove bark and to create decorative details. Follow the safety principles in the health and safety chapter.

Demonstrate and revise how to do a drawing of the product, labelling functional or decorative features.

Challenge 2 (in pairs or groups of four)

Join four sticks to create a frame

The children source their own materials (sticks from the ground, tools and/or string) to create their own frame structure, using joining techniques and adding detail to make it functional or appealing to match the design brief, with adult support as required. They then evaluate their product.

They draw their designs onto paper, drawing from different angles and adding labelling to show materials, joining techniques, measurements and functional or decorative features, to show other makers how to create their product.

PLENARY

The children discuss with a partner how they will continue to research decorative details and where their product could be placed.

EVALUATION/FOLLOW ON

- What went well and why?
- What didn't go as well as expected?
- What could be changed?
- Who stood out and why?

PREPARATION

Source the location of suitable parallel structures (some of which may have bracing), such as a ledged and braced door, decking, fencing, play equipment such as boats, rafts or bridge-type structures.

Source images of the same to show during the warm up.

Resources

- Images of parallel structures
- Variety of sticks
- Wire, wire-covered raffia or pipe cleaners
- String or cord
- Optional: scrap material for decoration
- Paper, pencils and clipboards
- Scissors
- Rulers
- Optional tool use: knives, rasps or peelers, safety gloves

Previous learning

Remind the children of the purpose of the Design and Technology sessions: they will be investigating, designing and building 'structures' to make a fantasy world for imaginative and creative writing for the school, utilising the outdoor learning area.

CONSIDER

Health & Safety

Assess and evaluate hazards and risks in your setting. See the health and safety chapter.

LESSON OBJECTIVES

We are exploring how parallel structures are designed, joined and strengthened.

National Curriculum Content

- Investigate and analyse a range of existing products.
- Select from and use a wider range of tools and equipment to perform practical tasks (for example, cutting, shaping, joining and finishing) accurately.
- Apply their understanding of how to strengthen, stiffen and reinforce more complex structures.

ADULT ROLES

- Support the whole task by encouraging careful observation.
- Ask questions about what the children can see and focus their observational skills.
- Support with tool skills but encourage the children to develop independence and cooperation, helping one another and demonstrating safe practice.

WARM UP IDEAS

Revise previous learning, finding out what the children have done with the products they have made. Share research and design ideas, including any illustrations of fantasy worlds, discussing how these might be applied to the outdoor learning area.

Inspect the outdoor learning area for suitable sites or settings for the fantasy structures. What criteria could they apply?

Introduce today's session structure focus on parallel structures, clarifying the terminology, and ask for examples of parallel structures – for example, a fence created by wood planks fixed next to one another to create a flat-faced structure – some of which may have bracing to strengthen and stabilise.

- Optional: Show an example of a model raft, bridge or other model, demonstrating how sticks have been placed next to one another to form a 'platform' or flat-faced structure, which can be used to illustrate the term 'parallel'.

Give other examples before asking the children to explore the setting environment, looking for existing parallel structures and products, and sketching them, noting details of their design.

Ask children to investigate their purpose, functional properties, material and construction, looking at joints, horizontal or diagonal bracing, etc., promoting understanding of joining, strengthening, stiffening and reinforcing.

MAIN ACTIVITIES

Parallel structures

Challenge 1 (groups of four)

Joining sticks in a parallel structure

Observe and practise a variety of joining techniques, exploring how materials can be strengthened or made more stable.

1. Model how to join five or six sticks into a 'raft' using wire weaving (raffia-covered wire or pipe cleaners). What makes it strong?

2. Model how to join four or five sticks with lashing ('under, over' across the width then 'over, under' back along the width).

3. Optional: If children are confident with knots, extend technical knowledge by introducing the marlinspike hitch knot (www.animatedknots.com/marlinspike-hitch-knot) or double floor lashing (https://scoutpioneering.com/videos/lashing-videos/floor-lashing).

Consider:

• What makes it strong?

• How can it be made stronger?

• Could more sticks be used to strengthen the structure in the form of doweling?

• Where and how would these be joined?

Now the structure has been made, what could it be? What additional detail would need to be added to make it functional or appealing to match the 'fantasy' brief? Take suggestions such as:

• A fantasy bridge – add uprights and string handrails then make a 'river' for it to cross.

• A raft – create a fantasy pond to float it, or add a mast using skills from Progression 1.

• A seat or throne – make it more comfortable or more ostentatious.

• A wall or roof for a fantasy structure – create sufficient products to make a walled or roofed structure. How will it stay up? How will it be joined? Does it have to be rectangular?

Optional tool use: Wearing safety gloves, model how to use knives, rasps or peelers to remove bark to create decorative details, following the step-by-step principles in the health and safety chapter.

Demonstrate how to do a drawing of the product from different angles, labelling key features.

Challenge 2 (individually or in pairs)

Using parallel structures to create products

The children source their own materials (sticks from the ground, tools and/or string) to create their own parallel structure, using joining techniques to create a stable product, with support as necessary.

They decide what their product could be, adding detail to make it functional or appealing to match the brief.

They draw their designs onto paper, labelling their drawing and showing materials, measurements and quantities, joining techniques and functional or decorative features, to clearly show other makers how to create their product. Are any modifications needed to make it fit the setting? What and why?

PLENARY

Children decide where in the setting their products could be placed. They explain what they have been doing and share what they have found out, discussing with a partner how they will continue to research decorative details.

EVALUATION/FOLLOW ON

• What went well and why?

• What didn't go as well as expected?

• What could be changed?

• Who stood out and why?

PREPARATION

Source the location of steps, curved or ladder-based structures, such as tree stumps, wood posts, block or tree stump steps, ladders, climbing frames, monkey bars, fencing, stepping stones, balustrade or balcony, etc.

Source images of the same to show during the introductory activity.

Resources

- Images of steps, curved or ladder-based structures
- Variety of sticks
- Wire, wire-covered raffia or pipe cleaners
- String or cord
- Optional: scrap material for decoration
- Paper, pencils and clipboards
- Scissors
- Rulers
- Optional tool use: knives, rasps or peelers, safety gloves

Previous learning

Remind the children of the purpose of the Design and Technology sessions: they will be investigating, designing and building structures to make a fantasy world in the outdoor learning area.

CONSIDER

Health & Safety

Assess and evaluate hazards and risks in your setting. See the health and safety chapter.

LESSON OBJECTIVES

We are exploring functional features of steps and parallel structures.

National Curriculum Content

- Investigate and analyse a range of existing products.
- Select from and use a wider range of tools and equipment to perform practical tasks (for example, cutting, shaping, joining and finishing) accurately.
- Apply their understanding of how to strengthen, stiffen and reinforce more complex structures.

ADULT ROLES

- Support the task by encouraging careful observation.
- Ask questions about what the children can see.
- Support with joining skills but encourage the children to develop independence and help one another.

WARM UP IDEAS

Share ideas of what the children now know about structures and how these might be applied to a fantasy world. Has anyone made any of the products at home, or brought them in to show and share?

Share the children's research and any plans that they have for the outdoor area to fulfil the brief of stimulating creative writing for the other children in the school (and themselves), exploring the area, explaining possible plans and deciding how the area meets the design criteria.

- What has changed?
- What is it about the areas that they have chosen?
- Why that area and not another?
- What do they need to consider, in relation to protecting the environment from harm or identifying potential hazards?

Introduce today's focus on steps and ladder-type structures, created by blocks of wood or parallel (wood) planks or bars with gaps between. What are the purpose and function of steps and ladders?

Give some examples before asking the children to explore the setting area looking for existing structures and products, and sketching them, noting details of their design.

Ask the children to investigate their purpose, functional properties, material and construction, looking at joints, bracing, etc., promoting understanding of how to join, strengthen, stiffen and reinforce more complex structures.

MAIN ACTIVITIES

Steps and ladders

Challenge 1 (whole class)

How to place or join sticks in a parallel structure

Observe and practise a variety of joining techniques, exploring how materials can be strengthened or made more stable.

- Model how to embed stumps, chunky sticks or branches (cut to different lengths using a saw) into the ground using a mallet.
- Model how to join five or six sticks onto two parallel longer sticks to create a fixed ladder structure using wire (raffia-covered wire or pipe cleaners) or lashing.
- Model how to join five or six sticks of the same length to two pieces of parallel rope using 'ladder lashing' to make a rope ladder.
- Consider what makes the structure strong, whether more sticks would strengthen it, as well as whether and how sticks could be added for another purpose, e.g. decoration.

Now the structure has been made, what could it be? What additional detail would need to be added to make it functional or appealing to match the 'fantasy' brief? Take suggestions such as:

- The embedded stumps could form a fence or narrow staircase.
- Place the ladders against a tree, a wall or down a hole, or attach them to a branch.

- Place the ladders horizontally as fantasy monkey bars or a scary rope bridge – suspending it from two branches or branch spurs.
- Place the ladder on its side (edge) to create a balcony rail; the rope version can be shaped or curved and attached to a tree.

Optional tool use: Wearing safety gloves, model how to use knives, rasps or peelers to remove bark or use marker pens or found objects to create decorative details. Use the step-by-step principles from the health and safety chapter.

Remind the children how to do a drawing of the product from different angles, labelling functional or decorative features.

Challenge 2 (individually or in pairs)

Making parallel structures

Children source and select their resources suiting their design (sticks from the ground, string and tools) to create their own structure, and use joining techniques to create a stable step or parallel structure, deciding what their product could be, with adult support as necessary.

They add detail to make it functional or appealing in order to meet the brief, before drawing their designs onto paper, showing materials, measurements, joining techniques and functional or decorative features. Did they need to make modifications? Does it fit the criteria?

PLENARY

Encourage the children to explain what they have been doing in the session and state what they have found out.

Back in the classroom

Explain that next time the children will be working in groups of six to eight to fulfil the design brief. They choose who will work with whom and agree roles.

They research and finalise their plans as a group, working on the different types of structure, e.g. crossbar, frame, parallel or ladder, so that each group fantasy world has structures of each type.

EVALUATION/FOLLOW ON

- What went well and why?
- What didn't go as well as expected?
- What could be changed?
- Who stood out and why?

PREPARATION

Source the location of a suitable fantasy world area within the setting.

Collect images of 'fantasy worlds' found by the pupils that would suit your setting resources and apply the learning from Progressions 1–4.

Resources

- Images of fantasy worlds
- Paper, pencils and clipboards
- Rulers
- Optional: camera

Previous learning

Discuss different joining techniques, favourite structures and designs and new ideas.

CONSIDER

Health & Safety

Assess and evaluate hazards and risks in your setting. See the health and safety chapter.

LESSON OBJECTIVES

We are using and applying our learning to design structures to satisfy a 'fantasy world' brief.

National Curriculum Content

- Use research and develop design criteria to inform the design of innovative, functional, appealing products that are fit for purpose, aimed at particular individuals or groups.
- Generate, develop, model and communicate their ideas through discussion and annotated sketches.
- Select from and use a wider range of tools and equipment to perform practical tasks accurately.
- Select from and use a wider range of materials and components, according to their functional properties and aesthetic qualities.
- Evaluate their ideas and products against their own design criteria and consider the views of others to improve their work.
- Apply their understanding of how to strengthen, stiffen and reinforce more complex structures.

ADULT ROLES

- Support the whole task by encouraging careful observation.
- Ask questions about what the children can see.
- Support with tool and joining skills but encourage the children to develop independence and help one another.
- Acknowledge difficulties and model how they can be overcome and seen as learning opportunities, being positive about the management of the difficulty.

WARM UP IDEAS

Seat the children in their working party groups.

Remind them of the brief to design and make fantasy world structures such as mini buildings, bridges, steps, doors and windows leading to or reflecting fantasy worlds for use by the whole school for imaginative storytelling in the outdoor learning area.

Revise and refresh the meaning of the word 'fantasy' by asking the children to provide examples from their research, both as individuals and as working party groups.

What type of structures might they find in a fantasy world and what do they look like? Do they have examples? Discuss how these could be used for their setting, identifying particular designs from the research that demonstrate the prototype structures and products that the children have made in previous progressions.

Consider:

- The possible modifications to the designs depending on the setting or placement of their products
- Environmental impact (if any)
- Any adaptations they will make to prevent damage or disturbance

MAIN ACTIVITIES

Designing a fantasy world

Explain that this week they will be drawing their designs first, to plan and show their ideas for their product. This will help them to consider and source the materials and tools needed to complete the task.

Challenge 1 (groups of six to eight)

How will we show what it will look like?

Demonstrate how to choose a setting for the product, drawing the setting and then adding the chosen structure or product 'in situ', such as at the base of a tree, in a corner, against a wall, near a water source or hollow, etc., labelling measurements and showing supporting, functional and decorative features, perhaps as an enlargement to one side.

Digital technologies can also be used for this activity, e.g. by taking photographs of the setting and overlaying or superimposing their designs.

Challenge 2 (groups of six to eight)

Specify, design, draw and source materials for structures for a fantasy world

Children decide where to place their fantasy setting before designing it in detail, including measurements, strengthening elements, decorative features and resource list. Make sure that each group member has a role.

Include a work brief, showing the order of work, agreeing who does what and ensuring that everyone has a role and is included.

Encourage the children to add and draw additional detail, which can be done to one side of the plan as an enlargement, in order to match the 'fantasy' brief. The children could work as pairs within the group, with each pair being responsible for one structure.

Ideas could include the prototypes from the progressions, listed below, but achievable original ideas from the groups should be encouraged:

- Cross-based structures
- Frame-based structures
- Parallel structures
- Step- or ladder-based structures

Additional structures or techniques could include weaving strands of willow to form shapes (as described in Year 3 Maths Progression 6).

What details make it 'fantasy'? For example:

- Wonky roof or irregular-shaped structures
- Moss-covered house
- Strange decoration such as gargoyles or faces
- Jewels and mirrors that catch the eye
- Strange plants, objects, vines or fabric strips hanging from trees
- An elaboration of a hole in a tree or in the ground
- Steps leading to a closed door with runes or strange markings on it
- A closed and obscure window in a tree
- Mini steps leading to... ?

Decorative features could be sourced from the setting, such as moss and plants, perhaps a garden (wild, neat and formal or a watery glen), a cave, paving or sand, fencing, furniture, balconies, wonky roofs, people, faces in the trees, animals, etc.

How will these be joined? Can they be attached to a tree or wall and if so how?

Optional: the children could investigate which plants could grow in their chosen locations and suit their designs, such as mini wild strawberry plants, herbs such as thyme or oregano, ground cover plants such as stonewort, saxifrage, moss or dwarf camomile, or succulents.

PLENARY

Encourage the children to share their ideas in situ with different groups, evaluating their ideas against the design criteria and considering the views of others to improve their work.

Re-evaluate and make notes and adjustments accordingly.

EVALUATION/FOLLOW ON

- What went well and why?
- What didn't go as well as expected?
- What could be changed?
- Who stood out and why?

PREPARATION

Support the children to source the materials they might need for their fantasy world designs.

Resources

- These will vary according to the designs and requirements of the groups
- The design drawings and plans created by the children in Progression 5
- Optional tool use: knives, saw, rasps or peelers, safety gloves

CONSIDER

Health & Safety

Assess and evaluate hazards and risks in your setting. See the health and safety chapter.

LESSON OBJECTIVES

We are using and applying our learning to create structures for a fantasy world.

National Curriculum Content

- Generate, develop, model and communicate their ideas through discussion and annotated sketches.
- Select from and use a wider range of tools and equipment to perform practical tasks accurately.
- Select from and use a wider range of materials and components, according to their functional properties and aesthetic qualities.
- Evaluate their ideas and products against their own design criteria and consider the views of others to improve their work.
- Apply their understanding of how to strengthen, stiffen and reinforce more complex structures.

ADULT ROLES

- Support with whole task by encouraging careful observation.
- Ask questions about what the children can actually see and observe in order to identify possible solutions to problems.
- Support with tool and joining skills but encourage the children to develop independence and help one another.
- Acknowledge difficulties and model how they can be overcome and seen as learning opportunities, being positive about the management of the difficulty.

WARM UP IDEAS

In their working party groups, remind children of the brief of designing and building 'structures' to create a fantasy world, or perhaps doors and windows leading to or reflecting fantasy worlds, for use by the whole school for imaginative storytelling in the outdoor learning area.

Revise and refresh the meaning of the word 'fantasy' by asking the children to provide examples from their research, both as individuals and in working party groups, identified in their design plans.

What details have they planned to add to their designs to make it 'fantasy'?

Has anyone changed or modified their plans in the light of feedback from others or as a result of resources and materials?

Explore any changes and discuss how these might impact on the designs or resourcing.

Discuss how they have considered:

- Environmental impact (if any)
- Any adaptations they will make to prevent damage or disturbance

Making a fantasy world

Challenge 1 (in groups of six to eight)

Create their structures for a fantasy world, using and applying skills and knowledge from previous progressions

Children will have decided and agreed on where to place their 'world', and now have the opportunity to work as a group to follow their planned designs.

Explain that it is important to review progress frequently, and that it is acceptable to change plans as long as everyone knows and agrees why, what the new plan is and how roles may be changed, ensuring that everyone has a task and is involved.

Encourage the children to take particular care in the additional 'finishing' details to make the product functional or appealing in order to match the brief.

Optional: wearing safety gloves, use knives, saws, rasps or peelers to shape, cut or remove bark, to join or to add decorative details, using the safety principles from the health and safety chapter.

PLENARY

Encourage the children to share their ideas and products and evaluate what they have been doing in the session, answering questions such as:

- Is it the same as my original design and if not, how is it different?
- What problems did I have and how did I solve the problem?
- Which bit do I like most and why?
- Which bit am I most proud of and why?
- Which bit would I change next time and why?

Back in the classroom

The children invite Year 5 to visit their fantasy worlds. The Year 5 pupils could be asked to write stories inspired by the worlds.

EVALUATION/FOLLOW ON

- What went well and why?
- What didn't go as well as expected?
- What could be changed?
- Who stood out and why?

Languages (French)

In this unit, children will be focusing on French language skills, based on the content of the Key Stage 2 languages attainment targets identified in the 2014 National Curriculum for England. Using the outdoors setting, the children are introduced to the vocabulary and phrases used to meet and greet. They are introduced to the colours of the rainbow and numbers one to twelve. They use this vocabulary to sing songs, explore the outdoor area and play French games. The ideas can be used with younger age groups according to setting policy and practice or to reinforce existing foreign language learning in the context of the outdoors. The progressions focus on practising and applying oral language skills, with the expectation being that written elements will (not exclusively) be reinforced in the classroom.

To support inclusive practice or to extend learning, the space, task, equipment and people (STEP) approach is adopted throughout this unit. By changing the space, task, equipment or people, the activity can be made more challenging or easier to understand, enabling all pupils to take part in the activity, as explained in the assessment chapter.

The main activities offer opportunities for adult-directed whole-group and smaller-group work, as well as opportunities for individual exploration and experimentation where appropriate. Timings will vary according to your setting, pupil experience and the support available.

You may wish to record the activities using a camera.

Natural connections

- Knowledge of local wildlife
- Tree and plant identification
- Care for the environment.

Health and wellbeing

- Physical activity
- Teamwork
- Self-regulation
- Independence.

Word bank

Meet and greet

- Bonjour!
- Je m'appelle...
- Au revoir
- Comment t'appelles-tu?
- Salut!
- Comment ça va?
- Ça va bien, merci
- Comme ci, comme ça
- Ça ne va pas
- Pas très bien

Numbers from one to 12 in French / Les nombres de 1 à 12 en français

- zéro
- un
- deux
- trois
- quatre
- cinq
- six
- sept
- huit
- neuf
- dix
- onze
- douze
- plus
- moins

The colours / Les couleurs

- rouge
- orange
- jaune
- vert
- bleu
- rose
- violet

Summary overview

Progression	Curriculum content	Learning experiences/activities
Lesson 1	Listen attentively to spoken language and show understanding by joining in and responding. Explore the patterns and sounds of language through songs. Engage in conversations; ask and answer questions.	Children learn to introduce themselves by name, to say hello and goodbye – 'Bonjour! Je m'appelle... Au revoir!' – and use this vocabulary to learn and say or sing the song *Deux Petits Oiseaux*. They make two birds out of sticks and clay with a partner and say or sing the song to one another.
Lesson 2	Speak in sentences, using familiar vocabulary, phrases and basic language structures. Present ideas and information orally.	Children revise the greetings and sing or say the *Deux Petits Oiseaux* song. They are introduced to the phrase 'Comment t'appelles-tu?', meaning 'What is your name?' or literally 'What do you call yourself?' They write the names of famous people on leaves and play the 'big question' name game, before re-singing the *Deux Petits Oiseaux* song. The Big Question activity links to Year 2 RE Progression 1.
Lesson 3		Children revise the greetings and sing or say the *Deux Petits Oiseaux* song. They introduce themselves, say an informal hello to a partner using 'Salut' and ask 'How are you?'. They go on a minibeast hunt in the outdoor area, finding and naming *les petites bêtes*.
Lesson 4		Children revise and reinforce learning about *les petites bêtes* from the previous progression. They learn colours and answer questions about what colour something is. They sing the colours of the rainbow in French. They go on an 'I spy' colour hunt, identifying the colours in the outdoor learning area.
Lesson 5		Children revise and reinforce prior learning by singing or saying *Deux Petits Oiseaux* and the colour names from previous progressions by singing the rainbow song. They are introduced to the numbers one to 12 by Monsieur Escargot and use these to play *l'escargot* hopscotch game.
Lesson 6		Children revise and reinforce number learning from the previous progression by playing a parachute numbers game. They learn to play boules and *le bilboquet* (the cup and ball), measuring distances or number of catches using numbers one to 12.

PREPARATION

Prepare the cue cards.

Source, record and practise *Deux Petits Oiseaux* song (available on YouTube, Vimeo, etc.).

Resources

- Cue cards with key French vocabulary, supported by pictures or photos as necessary
- Optional: means of playing the song, such as a portable speaker
- Clay, sticks and leaves

Previous learning

These progressions introduce the children to the French language and assume no prior experience. For those children who may have prior experience, these progressions can be used to reintroduce, practise and reinforce existing learning in the context of the outdoors.

CONSIDER

Health & Safety

Assess and evaluate hazards and risks in your setting. See the health and safety chapter.

LESSON OBJECTIVES

We are learning to say our names in French and say 'hello' and 'goodbye'.

National Curriculum Content

- Listen attentively to spoken language and show understanding by joining in and responding.
- Explore the patterns and sounds of language through songs.
- Present ideas and information orally.

ADULT ROLES

- Allow time for children to process their questions and answers. Come back to them if necessary.
- Model the language and support with images, sign language or gesture clues.

WARM UP IDEAS

Explain that for the next six sessions, the children will be learning French in the outdoor learning area. They will be asking questions, listening to answers, learning the French names of outdoor objects, learning French songs and playing French games. Today they will be learning how to say their names in French and to say 'hello' and 'goodbye' and use these words to learn and sing a song (or poem).

Introductory activity

In pairs, children move around the area shaking hands. As they shake hands, they take it in turns to say (in English), 'Hello, my name is… ', before waving to one another and saying (in English), 'Goodbye!' and finding another partner.

Alternatively, introduce the 'thumb stacker' handshake:

1. In pairs, one person puts out their left hand in a fist with the thumb up.
2. The partner holds their partner's thumb with their left hand (also making a fist with their own thumb sticking up).
3. Partner one holds onto the sticking up thumb with their right hand and finally partner two completes the stack by holding onto that thumb with their right hand.
4. The handshake can either go up and down or horizontally (like cutting down a tree with a saw).
5. As they shake hands, they take it in turns to say (in English), 'Hello, my name is… ', before waving to one another and saying (in English), 'Goodbye!' and finding another partner.

Bonjour!

Tell the children that you are going to introduce them to the words needed to do the same activity as the warm up, but in French.

Introduce the vocabulary on the cue cards with translation and actions:

- 'Bonjour!' (Shake hands with a child and wave hello.)
- Explain how the children can introduce themselves in French by saying *Je m'appelle* ('I am called') followed by their name.
- 'Au revoir!' (Wave goodbye.)

Explain that they can say their names in English.

Challenge 1 (in pairs)

Say hello, introduce themselves and say goodbye in French

Model a conversation with one of the children, using the vocabulary introduced above: *Bonjour, Je m'appelle...* and *Au revoir*. The children then hold the same conversation with a partner.

Challenge 2 (whole class)

Learn and sing the song *Deux Petits Oiseaux* using key vocabulary

Introduce and sing the song *Deux Petits Oiseaux* (or say it as a poem), adding your own gestures:

Deux petits oiseaux

Assis sur une branche *(Sitting on a branch)*

Je m'appelle Fifi

Je m'appelle Blanche

Bonjour Fifi

Bonjour Blanche

Au revoir Fifi

Au revoir Blanche

Challenge 3 (in pairs and whole class)

Make two simple bird models using clay, sticks and leaves and rehearse the poem to one another

Children explore the area, looking for found objects to add to a clay ball to create bird models representing Fifi and Blanche, chanting and singing the song as they do so.

They use the models to support a group performance of the song.

Encourage the children to explain what they have been doing in the session and state what they have learned.

- What went well and why?
- What didn't go as well as expected?
- What could be changed?
- Who stood out and why?

PREPARATION

Prepare the cue cards to include new vocabulary.

Leaves may need to be collected prior to the progression for drying.

Resources

- Cue cards with key French vocabulary, supported by pictures or photos as necessary
- Permanent markers
- A selection of dry leaves to write on
- Optional: Labels, dry leaves or wooden discs
- Optional: means of playing the song, such as a portable speaker

CONSIDER

Health & Safety

Assess and evaluate hazards and risks in your setting. See the health and safety chapter.

LESSON OBJECTIVES

We are practising greetings and goodbyes and learning how to ask someone their name.

National Curriculum Content

- Listen attentively to spoken language and show understanding by joining in and responding.
- Explore the patterns and sounds of language through songs.
- Engage in conversations; ask and answer questions.
- Speak in sentences, using familiar vocabulary, phrases and basic language structures.
- Present ideas and information orally.

ADULT ROLES

- Allow time for children to process their questions and answers. Come back to them if necessary.
- Model the language, reinforced with images, sign language or gesture.

WARM UP IDEAS

Explain that in this session the children will see what they can remember from the last session by playing the handshake introduction activity and singing *Deux Petits Oiseaux*.

Tell them that in this session they will learn how to ask 'What is your name?', before playing a name game.

Introductory activity

Revision of previous learning

In pairs, children move around the area shaking hands, or repeat the 'thumb stacker' handshake activity from Progression 1.

As they shake hands, they take it in turns to say: 'Bonjour! Je m'appelle... Au revoir!'

Remind them that they can say their names in English. You could translate the children's names into French if possible, such as Peter/Pierre, Wadi/Ouadie, Eliza/Elise, etc.

These names could be written onto a label or leaf and attached to the child's clothing, or onto a wooden disc, or peeled stick, decorated and made into a necklace, but allow additional time for this activity.

MAIN ACTIVITIES

What's your name?

Tell the children that you are going to introduce them to the French words needed to ask someone their name: 'Comment t'appelles-tu?' (What are you called?). Show them the cue cards.

Challenge 1 (in pairs)

Say hello, introduce themselves, ask a partner's name and say goodbye in French

Model a conversation with one of the children, as follows:

1. Shake hands with a partner and say 'Bonjour!'
2. 'Je m'appelle... Comment t'appelles-tu?'
3. Child responds with 'Je m'appelle... ' (giving their own name).
4. 'Au revoir!' (Both wave goodbye.)

Ask the children to try the same with a partner of their own, repeating the activity by finding new partners and taking it in turns to ask the question: 'Comment t'appelles-tu?'

Challenge 2 (whole class in pairs)

Play the famous name 'big question' game

Ask the children to collect two dry leaves each and write the names of famous people on each one.

Play the big question game with them.

1. Each child has a famous name leaf.
2. They find a partner and take turns to each ask one another, 'Comment t'appelles-tu?'
3. The person who has been asked responds with: 'Je m'appelle... ', giving the name on the leaf.
4. They swap names and find new partners to ask.

Challenge 3 (whole class)

Sing *Deux Petits Oiseaux* with actions

Can they improve their performance?

PLENARY

Encourage the children to explain what they have been doing in the session and state what they have learned.

EVALUATION/FOLLOW ON

- What went well and why?
- What didn't go as well as expected?
- What could be changed?
- Who stood out and why?

PREPARATION

Prepare the cue cards to include new vocabulary.

Prepare minibeast cue cards with pictures and French names.

Prepare a minibeast hunt sheet in French with supporting images (or these can be drawn by the children, linking to Year 3 art). A supporting worksheet can be found at the back of this book.

Resources

- Cue cards with key French vocabulary, supported by pictures or photos as necessary
- *Les petites bêtes* cue cards
- *Les petites bêtes* sheets (illustrated)
- Toy or model snail or other minibeast
- Pencils and clipboards
- Optional: means of playing the song, such as a portable speaker

Previous learning

This progression links to Year 3 science progressions.

CONSIDER

Health & Safety

Assess and evaluate hazards and risks in your setting. See the health and safety chapter.

LESSON OBJECTIVES

We are learning to ask someone how they are and how to respond. We are hunting for *les petites bêtes*.

National Curriculum Content

- Listen attentively to spoken language and show understanding by joining in and responding.
- Engage in conversations; ask and answer questions.
- Speak in sentences, using familiar vocabulary, phrases and basic language structures.
- Present ideas and information orally.

ADULT ROLES

- Allow time for children to process their questions and answers. Come back to them if necessary.
- Model the language, reinforced with images, sign language or gesture.

WARM UP IDEAS

Explain that in this session children will see what they can remember from the last session by playing the handshake introduction activity, singing *Deux Petits Oiseaux* and asking one another what their names are.

State that today they will learn to ask one another how they are, before going on a minibeast hunt in the outdoor area.

Introductory activity

Children move around the outdoor learning area. Shaking hands, they greet one another with 'Bonjour! Comment t'appelles-tu?' and respond with 'Bonjour, je m'appelle... ', before both giving a cheery wave goodbye with an 'Au revoir!'.

They sing and perform *Deux Petits Oiseaux* with actions.

MAIN ACTIVITIES

How are you? *Les petites bêtes*

Tell the children that you are going to introduce them, using the cue cards, to the French words needed to ask someone you know well, or are friends with, how they are: 'Comment ça va?' (formal) or simply 'Ça va?' (informal).

Explain that the response could be:

- Ça va bien, merci (all good, thank you – with a smile or thumbs up).
- Comme ci, comme ça (okay-ish or so, so – with an inclined head and hovering hand).
- Ça ne va pas (not good! I'm not fine – with a thumbs down and a grumpy facial expression).
- Pas très bien (not very well – looking sad).

At this point, it could be explained that in French there are different ways of saying hello to friends, just as in English – like Hi, Hello, etc. *Salut* can be introduced as an informal greeting, since the children know one another well now.

Challenge 1 (in pairs)

Ask a partner how they are and the partner responds

Teacher to model the whole conversation, as follows:

1. Salut!
2. Comment ça va?
3. Ça va bien, merci/Comme ci, comme ça/Ça ne va pas/Pas très bien (in a different voice or modelled with another adult, with appropriate expressions).
4. Can the children understand? Ask them to translate.

Ask the children to try the same with a partner of their own, repeating the activity by finding new partners and taking it in turns to ask the question 'Comment ça va?' and varying their replies.

Challenge 2 (whole class and individual)

Exploring living things in the outdoor area

Introduce a model or toy snail or other creature that might be found in the outdoor learning area habitat, by saying its name in English. Then say 'Bonjour!'.

Prompt the children to ask the creature: 'Comment t'appelles-tu?', then respond by saying 'Je m'appelle Monsieur [say the name of the creature you've chosen in French, e.g. Escargot for snail]. They respond, 'Bonjour Monsieur Escargot'.

Monsieur Escargot tells the children: 'J'habite dans le jardin' – what could he mean?

Translate for the children, i.e. 'I live in the garden' (change this to suit your outdoor area).

In English, reinforce and revise previous learning about habitats, with questions such as: Where do snails like to live? What habitat do they prefer?

You ask Monsieur Escargot: 'Quels animaux habitent dans le jardin?'

Can the children guess what you said?

Translate for the children, i.e. 'What animals live in the garden?'

What animals do they know?

Show the cue cards with the minibeasts and their French names.

Ask the children to repeat the names as you show the cards. Repeat.

Explain that the children will be exploring the garden looking for *les petites bêtes*.

Hand out *les petites bêtes* sheets, pencils and clipboards. The children go off on their hunt. How many can they find and can they say the French minibeast names when they are found?

PLENARY

Encourage the children to explain what they have been doing in the session and state what they have learned. Where was the best place to find *les petites bêtes*?

EVALUATION/FOLLOW ON

- What went well and why?
- What didn't go as well as expected?
- What could be changed?
- Who stood out and why?

PREPARATION

Prepare the cue cards to include new vocabulary.

Source, record and learn the *Rainbow Song* in English and French.

Prepare colour collection sheets in French as below.

Les couleurs

Couleurs	Tally
Rouge (red)	
Jaune (yellow)	
Rose (pink)	
Vert (green)	
Violet (purple)	
Orange (orange)	
Bleu (blue)	

Resources

- Cue cards with colour and *les petites bêtes* vocabulary, supported by pictures or photos as necessary
- Paint shade cards (available online)
- Colour collection sheets – *les feuilles (f) de couleur*
- Pencils and clipboards
- Optional: means of playing the song, such as a portable speaker

Previous learning

Children may have previously explored colours in the outdoor learning area.

CONSIDER

Health & Safety

Assess and evaluate hazards and risks in your setting. See the health and safety chapter.

LESSON OBJECTIVES

We are learning the colours of the rainbow and hunting for colours in the outdoor learning area.

National Curriculum Content

- Listen attentively to spoken language and show understanding by joining in and responding.
- Explore the patterns and sounds of language through songs.
- Engage in conversations; ask and answer questions.
- Speak in sentences, using familiar vocabulary, phrases and basic language structures.
- Present ideas and information orally.

ADULT ROLES

- Allow time for children to process their questions and answers. Come back to them if necessary.
- Model the language, reinforced with images, sign language or gesture.

WARM UP IDEAS

Explain that in this session, the children will see what they can remember from the last progressions by identifying *les petites bêtes*, and their new learning will be the colours in a rainbow.

Do they know what colours there are in a rainbow in English? How do they remember the colours in English? Do they know any mnemonics, such as Richard Of York Gave Battle In Vain? Do they know of any songs that help them remember the colours?

How many colours can the children name in English? Revise and repeat.

Sing the first verse of the Rainbow Song in English:

Red and yellow and pink and green, purple and orange and blue.

I can sing a rainbow, sing a rainbow, sing a rainbow too.

Introductory activity

What am I? What do you call yourself?

Holding up *les petites bêtes* cards one at a time, ask the question: 'Comment t'appelles-tu?'

MAIN ACTIVITIES

Rainbow colours

Tell the children that you are going to introduce them to the French words needed to name the colours of the rainbow.

This session could reintroduce 'Monsieur Escargot' (or whoever your character in Progression 3, Challenge 2 was). The children say hello: 'Bonjour, Monsieur Escargot!' Can they sing the English version of the *Rainbow Song* to him?

Challenge 1 (whole class)

Learn the colours of the rainbow in French

Show the cue cards and introduce the colours: 'Quelle est cette couleur?' (What colour is this?)

- Rouge (red)
- Orange (orange)
- Jaune (yellow)
- Vert (green)
- Violet (purple)
- Rose (pink)
- Bleu (blue)

They learn and sing the (adapted for scanning) *Rainbow Song* in French:

Rouge et jaune et rose et vert

Violet, orange et bleu

Je connais les couleurs,

Toutes les couleurs,

Celles de l'arc-en-ciel.

Challenge 2 (individual)

Exploring colours in the outdoor area

Explain that the children will be exploring the outdoor learning area and using a colour card to collect as many colours as they can.

Hand out *la feuille de couleur*, pencils and clipboards and go on an 'I spy' colour hunt, identifying the colours in the outdoor learning area. How many colours can they find and name when found?

Alternatively, use a paint shade card with double-sided tape stuck along its length and collect colours from the area by sticking colour matched flowers, leaves and other found objects onto the card.

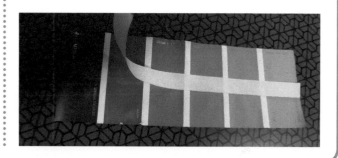

PLENARY

Encourage the children to explain what they have been doing in the session and state what they have learned. Did anything surprise them? What was the most common colour? Can they say the colour in French?

Back in the classroom

Decide how to display their findings about the colours they found, e.g. in a bar chart.

EVALUATION/FOLLOW ON

- What went well and why?
- What didn't go as well as expected?
- What could be changed?
- Who stood out and why?

PREPARATION

Prepare number cue cards or adapt number fans with number names in French.

Draw a large spiral snail shell on the ground in chalks (big enough to stand on). Divide it into squares and add the numbers one to twelve.

Resources

- Cue cards with previous key French vocabulary, supported by pictures or photos as necessary
- Number cue cards
- Chalks
- Optional: means of playing the song, such as a portable speaker.

CONSIDER

Health & Safety

Assess and evaluate hazards and risks in your setting. See the health and safety chapter.

LESSON OBJECTIVES

We are learning the numbers one to twelve and using these to play *la marelle escargot* (snail hopscotch).

National Curriculum Content

- Listen attentively to spoken language and show understanding by joining in and responding.
- Explore the patterns and sounds of language through songs.
- Engage in conversations; ask and answer questions.
- Speak in sentences, using familiar vocabulary, phrases and basic language structures.
- Present ideas and information orally.

ADULT ROLES

- Allow time for children to process their questions and answers. Come back to them if necessary.
- Model the language, reinforced with images, sign language or gesture.

WARM UP IDEAS

Explain that today the children will be introduced to the numbers one to twelve by Monsieur Escargot and use these to play a game called *la marelle escargot*, a form of hopscotch. Clarify their understanding of hopscotch rules and how to play.

Introductory activity

1. Sing the song *Deux Petits Oiseaux*.
2. 'Quelle est cette couleur?' Sing the *Rainbow Song*, holding up the appropriate colour cue cards as they sing.
3. Then, holding up *les petites bêtes* cue cards (from Progression 3) one at a time, ask the question: 'Comment t'appelles-tu?' How many can the children name? Revise and repeat.

Les nombres

Tell the children that you are going to introduce them to the French words needed to count up to 12.

Reintroduce Monsieur Escargot. 'Bonjour Monsieur Escargot!'

Challenge 1 (whole class)

Learn the numbers one to twelve in French

Show the cue cards and introduce the numbers zero to twelve.

This can be done as a song, such as adapting the 'ABCDEFG' alphabet song, or by the children standing in a circle (this can be demarcated using a rope or webbing) and jumping in in turn, calling out the numbers in French.

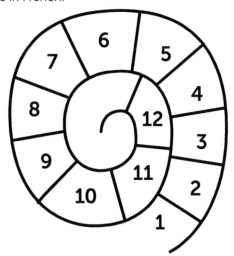

Challenge 2 (in pairs or groups of four)

Exploring numbers in the outdoor area

Show the children the chalk-drawn snail shell with number squares.

Does it remind any of them of another game they know?

Like hopscotch, players take turns to hop on one foot all the way to the centre spot and back out again. Their foot must not touch any of the lines.

If they succeed, they write their initials inside a number square using chalk. They must say the number that they have chosen out loud in French.

The next person to hop must avoid any squares with initials drawn inside them, by hopping over these squares.

The game continues until it is impossible to reach the centre.

Encourage the children to explain what they have been doing in the session and state what they have learned. How easy was the hopscotch game? Could they play it at break time too? Could they teach it to a child from a different class?

- What went well and why?
- What didn't go as well as expected?
- What could be changed?
- Who stood out and why?

PREPARATION

Source the boules or equivalent.

Source the *bilboquet* (cup and ball) or resources to make these in the session, e.g. skewers, paper or polystyrene cups, lengths of string or wool, large wooden or plastic beads with a hole through them (or recycle a lemon juice holder), and make a prototype to show the children.

Resources

- Cue cards with numbers vocabulary
- Optional: parachute, colourful if possible
- Boules, or, if not available, cricket balls and golf balls
- Cup and ball or the materials to make them (see Preparation)
- Chalk
- Optional: means of playing the song, such a portable speaker

CONSIDER

Health & Safety

Assess and evaluate hazards and risks in your setting. See the health and safety chapter.

LESSON OBJECTIVES

We are learning to use the numbers one to twelve to play French games (*la marelle escargot*, *bilboquet* and boules).

National Curriculum Content

- Listen attentively to spoken language and show understanding by joining in and responding.
- Engage in conversations; ask and answer questions.
- Speak in sentences, using familiar vocabulary, phrases and basic language structures.
- Present ideas and information orally.

ADULT ROLES

- Allow time for children to process their questions and answers. Come back to them if necessary.
- Model the language, reinforced with images, sign language or gesture.

WARM UP IDEAS

Tell the children that in this session they will be using what they have learned in previous sessions to play French games.

Introductory activity

Whole class

Sing the numbers song to secure and reinforce children's prior learning, then introduce the parachute game – based on the game 'fruit salad'. Note that this game can be played without a parachute if you don't have access to one.

1. Each child holds the parachute at waist level and identifies the colours that are nearest to them by giving the French name.
2. Each child is given a number one to twelve (in French).
3. The children raise and lower the parachute, practising making a 'mushroom'. The parachute at its highest should be high enough for children to be underneath without it touching them.
4. Call a number in French, such as 'deux' and all the 'twos' swap places by running under the parachute to take each other's places.
5. Repeat with different numbers.
6. As an additional challenge, this activity could be linked to maths by using 'plus' or 'moins' to make simple calculations, such as: 'deux et trois font?' (two and three make) and number fives swap places. Allow processing time for this.

MAIN ACTIVITIES

Number games

Tell the children that you are going to introduce them to French games that use numbers. They learn to play boules and *bilboquet* (cup and ball), measuring distances or number catches using numbers one to 12.

Practise number and colour learning by playing boules, *la marelle escargot* and *bilboquet*

The children will be practising their numbers by playing one or more of three games. Remind them about the escargot game from Progression 5. Show the children how to play boules and *bilboquet*. The children choose who they want to play with and which games they want to play.

Challenge 1 (groups of four)

Play boules

1. Choose a firm surface such as gravel and use sticks to mark the boundary of the play area.
2. Decide on the teams and choose a coloured ball (if using cricket balls, use a coloured sticker to identify the team).
3. Decide who in the team goes first.
4. This person marks a circle on the ground to be the base, which everyone must be in to play their boule.
5. This person throws the jack (the small ball).
6. Both teams throw a boule as close to the jack as they can. The team that get nearest then continue to throw their boules until everyone has been.
7. The other team then throw their boules.
8. The team with the most boules nearest the jack wins.
9. Use a measuring tape to see who is closest. Say the numbers in French.

Challenge 2 (individual)

Make and play *bilboquet*

1. Make the cup and ball game by making a small hole in the base of the cup with the skewer.
2. Tie a knot in the end of the string and pass this through the hole, with the knot on the inside. Secure this with masking tape.
3. Tie the bead to the other end of the string (or unscrew the lemon juice container lid, wrap the string around it and replace the lid).
4. The children now have their bilboquets!
5. Play the game by seeing how many times the bead can be swung gently up to land in the cup, counting the number in French.

Challenge 3 (in pairs or groups of four)

La marelle escargot

See Challenge 2 from Progression 5.

PLENARY

Encourage the children to explain what they have been doing in the lesson and state what they have learned. How confident do they feel about meeting and greeting in French, playing games and using numbers? Can they remember any minibeast names? Which name stands out and is easily remembered? Why might this be? Sing the *Rainbow Song*.

EVALUATION/FOLLOW ON

- What went well and why?
- What didn't go as well as expected?
- What could be changed?
- Who stood out and why?

Music

In this unit, 'dynamic musicians' are created as children tune in to the sounds of nature. Children are encouraged to investigate 'nature's orchestra' by listening to the sounds around them in outdoor soundscapes, imitating what they have heard and composing their own music inspired by the sounds of nature. The use of vocabulary linked to the dynamics of music is integral to the unit. The children will also explore sounds that can be created using natural and man-made objects. They will improvise and compose their own music using instruments made of recycled junk, forming their own junk band. They will also develop their own soundscape through the 'garden of sound'. The skill of listening runs throughout the unit as pupils listen with attention to detail and recall sounds with increasing aural memory. The children get the opportunity to perform in an outdoor musical festival, 'The Wild Side', which enables them to express and show off their musical talents.

Prior to starting this unit, you may wish to start a sound collection box in the school and encourage parents, children and the community to donate unwanted instruments and junk items.

To support inclusive practice or to extend learning, the space, task, equipment and people (STEP) approach can be adopted throughout this unit. By changing the space, task, equipment or people, the activity can be made more challenging or easier to understand, enabling all pupils to take part in the activity, as explained in the assessment chapter in this book.

You may wish to record the activities using a camera.

Natural connections

- Exploring the local environment
- Identifying and appreciating natural sounds
- Tuning into the local soundscape.

Health and wellbeing

- Listening
- Physical activity
- Teamwork
- Self-regulation and independence
- Risk management
- Creativity
- Confidence.

Word bank

Percussion
The striking of one solid object with or against another; instruments whose sound is created by striking / hitting them

Orchestra
A large group of musicians who play together

Conduct / conductor
The lead of an ensemble (group) of musicians, who gives directions using their hands or a baton (stick)

Beat
A rhythmic pulse; the speed at which a piece of music is played

Dynamics
The loudness or softness of sound

Crescendo / diminuendo
Getting louder / getting quieter

Tempo
The speed of the beat

Compose / composition
To create a piece of music / a piece of music

Soundscape
A collection of individual sounds within a given environment

Presto / lento
A rapid speed / a slow speed

Accelerando / ritardando
Speeding up / slowing down

Pulse
Steady underlying beat

Rhythm
Patterns of long and short notes or rests (intervals of silence)

Texture / timbre
How many instruments / voices, rhythms and pitches make up the overall piece/quality of sound

Summary overview

Progression	Curriculum content	Learning experiences/activities
Lesson 1	The series of progressions across Key Stage 2 music all address the following curriculum content: Play and perform in solo and ensemble contexts, using their voices and playing musical instruments with increasing accuracy, fluency, control and expression. Improvise and compose music for a range of purposes, using the interrelated dimensions of music. Listen with attention to detail and recall sounds with increasing aural memory.	**Sound clips of nature:** Children will listen to and identify sounds within an outdoor soundscape, playing the game 'Secret sound'. They will then have the opportunity to record and create their own 'sound clips' and create a sound map for the school. They will need to listen with attention to detail as they recall the sounds and identify the source.
Lesson 2		**The rhythm of sound:** Children explore the potential of the natural world to provide rhythmic and percussion sounds, then use tools to make an instrument from natural materials – a 'nature instrument'. They become 'dynamic duos' as they experiment with dynamics (loudness/softness) of sound. They create a sound trail through the discovery and description of found sounds.
Lesson 3		**Body percussion:** Children explore percussion, beat, tempo, orchestra and conducting, using body percussions to create rhythm compositions as a body percussion orchestra. With a 'musical buddy', they compose and perform a short body percussion composition reflecting the natural world. They create a 'sound slide' to overlay natural objects, words, voices, movement and body percussion.
Lesson 4		**The garden of sound:** The children take part in a musical challenge to identify a range of different sounds in the outdoor area. They then improvise and make a range of items to develop a 'garden of sound', including a stage, listening pod, sound trail and music wall.
Lesson 5		**The junk band:** Children continue to explore, improvise and compose as they develop their own musical instruments by recycling junk, and compose a musical piece performing in a junk band in the 'garden of sound'.
Lesson 6		**Music festival – 'Music on the Wild Side':** In this final session, children perform. They use the 'garden of sound' as an outdoor venue. They decide which songs they will sing, how they will use the junk band performances and how they can use other musical talent in the class to play and perform in solo and ensemble contexts. Children should be encouraged to play musical instruments they have made or instruments they are learning to play to improve their accuracy, fluency and expression in music.

PREPARATION

Prepare a recording of six to eight sounds, both from natural and artificial sources (e.g. birds or machines) for the 'Secret sounds' activity.

Make a basic map of the school grounds. Note: younger children may need to follow an exemplar map with sound points already on it prior to creating their own; create this if applicable.

Ensure that the children have access to a natural environment for this session in which they can listen to a variety of sounds.

Resources

- www.scoutresources.org.uk/SR/songs/index.html
- 'Secret sounds' recorded on a tablet or other device
- Card or paper, permanent markers and pencils
- Maps of the school grounds, enough for one per pair
- Wooden discs
- Tablets or other recording devices, enough for one per pair

Previous learning

This session reinforces the geography progressions (using orienteering and map-work).

CONSIDER

Health & Safety

Assess and evaluate hazards and risks in your setting. See the health and safety chapter.

LESSON OBJECTIVES

We are learning to create sound clips using sounds from nature and identify sounds within our outdoor soundscape.

National Curriculum Content

- Listen with attention to detail and recall sounds with increasing aural memory.

ADULT ROLES

- Encourage a 'have a go' approach and to ask for help when it's needed.
- Model how to listen, describe and identify.

WARM UP IDEAS

Tune in

Explain to the children that through this unit they will be exploring the sounds of nature. They will have the opportunity to compose their own music and make their own instruments from natural items.

Singing school

Start this session by singing a song that the children know. This could include songs accompanied by percussion or percussive noises, e.g. *If you're happy and you know it*, or campfire songs, e.g. *She'll be coming round the mountain, You'll never get to heaven* or *London's burning*, which could be sung in rounds. See the resources section for further ideas.

Introductory activity

Talk to the children about the sounds of nature.

- What sounds can they hear in the outdoor learning area?
- What sounds could they create using natural objects?
- Ask the children to find two items in the area that they can use to make a noise.
- Share the sounds with a partner.

Secret sound

- Give the children a piece of card and a pencil and ask them to write the numbers one to eight as a vertical list. Explain that this is their secret sound answer card.
- Play the children the pre-recorded sounds (see preparation).
- Can they guess the sounds? Write each one down in turn.
- Which sounds are easy to identify? Which require further listening and analysis? Why is this?

MAIN ACTIVITIES

Sound bites of nature

Introducing the terminology of sound

Talk to the children about sounds. Clarify and define the meaning of 'sound', 'soundscape' and 'sound clip'.

- A sound is vibrations through the air, which can be heard by the ear.
- A soundscape is a collection of sounds within a given environment.
- A sound clip is a short clip from a longer sound or piece of music.

Challenge 1 (in pairs)

Creating a soundscape map using sound clips

Note: younger children may need to follow an exemplar map modelled by the teacher prior to creating their own map.

Tell the children that they will now be given the opportunity to create their own sound clip using a tablet or other recording device.

- Give the children a map of the school grounds, explaining that they will use this to mark the location of each listening spot used for their sound bite, e.g. if they record a sound clip in the corner of the football field, they will mark the location with 'sound clip' on the map, along with a number.
- Explain that they will need to identify at least six points on the map where they can record their own sound clips, first checking that it is possible to record a sound at each point.
- Give the children wooden discs. They leave one disc at each point they record a sound, giving each one a different number.
- Explain that they will need to come up with a symbol to represent the sound that has been recorded. These will be drawn on the wooden discs.
- Make sure that the children create a master answer sheet, recording which symbol has been left at which point on the map, e.g. 1 – corner of football field, bird call, bird symbol, as they will be giving their map to another pair.

- Once the children have recorded all their sound clips. Talk to the children about the sounds they have recorded. They have created their own soundscape by using a map and recording their own sounds.

Challenge 2 (in pairs)

'Go find it' sound hunt

Using a map and the recorded sound clips created by another pair, the children go and find the sounds on the sound map. They will need to identify the point on the map and then play the first sound clip to see whether they are correct. They will also need to collect the correct wooden disc from each sound point.

Once they have completed the challenge, talk to the children about their findings.

- Did they locate all the sounds from the sound map?
- What sounds did they hear?
- How many different sounds did they pick out?
- Can they name any of them?
- Compare and contrast: what sounds were similar/different? Pleasing/displeasing? How does the soundscape make them feel?

PLENARY

Talk to the children about the sounds they have heard in the session, the sound clips they have created and how they have used these to develop sound maps for the school.

EVALUATION/FOLLOW ON

- What went well today?
- Which children understood the concepts?
- Which children needed more help?
- Are there other resources you can use?
- Can the children use some of the sound clips created to develop a secret sound quiz back in the classroom?

PREPARATION

There are Italian words and abbreviations for different dynamics:

ff – *fortissimo*, very loud;

f – *forte*, loud;

mf – *mezzo forte*, quite loud;

mp – *mezzo piano*, quite quiet;

p – *piano*, quiet;

pp – *pianissimo*, very quiet.

Write the word and abbreviation on one side of the wooden discs, and the English on the other.

Make two V-shaped sticks, one to be labelled and angled as *crescendo* (<), one as *diminuendo* (>).

Resources

- Percussion sticks (or other percussion) – one per child
- Six wooden discs and two V-shaped sticks with dynamic markings
- Rope and string
- Pegs

Previous learning

Revisit and review: What is percussion? What is a beat?

Build on singing school skills (Progression 1) by mimicking a conductor's set beat and percussion skills, working as part of an ensemble.

Links to geography (rope trail).

CONSIDER

Health & Safety

Assess and evaluate hazards and risks in your setting. See the health and safety chapter.

LESSON OBJECTIVES

We explore the dynamics of sound and create a sound trail and a musical instrument from natural objects.

National Curriculum Content

- Play and perform in solo and ensemble contexts, using their voices and playing musical instruments with increasing accuracy, fluency, control and expression.
- Improvise and compose music for a range of purposes, using the interrelated dimensions of music.

ADULT ROLES

- Encourage a 'have a go' approach and asking for help.
- Model how to listen, describe and identify.

WARM UP IDEAS

Exploring dynamics in pairs to become a 'dynamics duo'

Today we will be experimenting with the loudness and softness of sound.

1. Demonstrate how to sing the dynamic signature of a wooden disc. Ask the children to repeat.
2. One child (as the 'conductor') sings a dynamic signature name at the volume level it stands for by selecting a wooden disc from the sound box. The class repeat the name at the same volume, then another child becomes the 'conductor'.
3. When the children have used their voices using a variety of the wooden discs, introduce percussion sticks or other percussion.
4. Model how the conductor taps and speaks a beat, which their partner then repeats after them. The children have a go with their partner.
5. Introduce *crescendo* and *diminuendo* dynamics symbols, getting louder and quieter. Tap the sticks a total of 10 times, counting from one to ten and tapping, gradually increasing the volume of the taps and voice for *crescendo* and gradually decreasing the volume of the taps and voice for *diminuendo*.

Then explore and vary the tempo.

Examples of instruments made from natural materials.

MAIN ACTIVITIES

The rhythm of sound

Challenge 1 (in pairs)

The sound trail

Explain that the children will now create a sound trail by discovering and describing 'found' sounds.

Working in pairs, they find natural or man-made objects, which make a sound when touched or moved.

They create a sound trail by hanging objects from a rope with pegs, then try out each other's trails.

Challenge 2 (individuals and small groups)

Make a percussion stick

Tell the children they will now have the opportunity to make a percussion stick.

- Using tools following the health and safety chapter guidance, the children gather two sticks at least 2 cm in diameter and 10–15 cm in length, or cut sticks to this length.

- Saw a series of equally spaced notches about 2 cm apart and 1 cm deep along the middle section of the stick, placing the blade of the knife halfway between two of the vertical cuts and carving down towards the base of the next vertical notch. A rubber mallet can be used to help create the notches and remove the wood.

- Repeat this process along the stick to create a series of notches.

Let the children try it out, moving the un-notched stick forwards and backwards over the notches. In groups, can they create a rhythm using the stick? Can they create soft and loud sounds, fast and slow, using the dynamics and tempo of sound?

Extension activity (individual with adult support)

Creating a clacker rhythm stick

In this challenge, children will create clacker rhythm sticks using a sharp knife, saw and a palm drill.

- Following the safe tool-use principles, the children will need to select and cut a length of bough wood, ideally from a chestnut or ash tree. This will need to be at least 3–4 cm thick and 25–30 cm long.

- Working under the supervision of an adult, measure 15 cm in from the end and make a cut by sawing one third of the way through.

- Turn the wood a half turn and make another saw cut one third of the way through, opposite the first saw cut, and place the bough length upright on a drill stump.

- Place the knife on the top of the bough, aligning it with the saw cuts one third across the diameter, then cleave the wood down to the saw cut. This will remove a section from the main bough.

- Repeat the process on the other side of the wood by turning the piece of wood 180 degrees.

- You will be left with two rectangular pieces of wood, curved on one side, which will form the moving clacker parts, and the remaining bough, the uncut part of which will become the 'handle'.

- To reassemble the bough, drill two holes through the slender part of the bough and the bottom of the two 'clacker' parts, and reattach the two clacker parts by threading string through the holes, tightening as necessary to allow them to 'clack' together when shaken.

- If time allows, the bough can be stripped of bark and shaped using whittling.

PLENARY

Talk to the children about the sound trail they have created, their understanding of the dynamics of sound and how they have made a musical instrument from natural objects. What has worked well? What do they still need to improve with their instrument?

EVALUATION/FOLLOW ON

- What went well today?
- Which children understood the concepts?
- Which children needed more help?
- Are there other resources you can use?
- Can the children develop their instrument further back in the classroom?

PREPARATION

Access to a range of natural objects to create a 'sound slide'.

Create discs for the tempo markings *accelerando* and *ritardando* in the same way as for dynamics in Progression 5.

accel. – *accelerando*, get faster;

rit. – *ritardando*, get slower.

Resources

- A range of natural objects
- Two wooden discs with tempo markings
- https://pdst.ie/sites/default/files/Exploring%20sound%20body%20percussion.pdf

Previous learning

Build on previous session's learning of dynamics by incorporating a range of soft and loud sounds in a 'musical buddies' activity. Revise tempo as the speed of the beat.

CONSIDER

Health & Safety

Assess and evaluate hazards and risks in your setting. See the health and safety chapter.

LESSON OBJECTIVES

We can explore our bodies as a musical instrument and develop body percussion.

National Curriculum Content

- Play and perform in solo and ensemble contexts, using their voices and playing musical instruments with increasing accuracy, fluency, control and expression.
- Improvise and compose music for a range of purposes, using the interrelated dimensions of music.

ADULT ROLES

- Conduct – teaching, modelling, leading group ensemble work.
- Encourage a 'have a go' approach and to ask for help when it's needed.
- Model how to listen, describe and identify.

WARM UP IDEAS

Body percussion (whole class and in pairs)

Explain to the children that in this session they are exploring a variety of body sounds using their own bodies as instruments, creating rhythm compositions as a body percussion orchestra.

1. Model the following pattern with the children:
   - One hand clap
   - One double-handed chest thump
   - Two separate thigh slaps.
2. Repeat with the children now joining in, mimicking the adult-modelled body percussion.
3. Now ask the children to work in pairs. Can one member of the pair come up with a rhythm, which is repeated by the other child? Repeat twice and then swap over.
   - Can they now tap out their names in a rhythm to add to the sequence?
   - Can they build up the composition with six sounds using MTYT (my turn, your turn)?
4. Introduce two tempo word discs: *accelerando* (speeding up) and *ritardando* (slowing down).
5. Can they include this in their body percussion sequence?
6. For further ideas, see the resources section.

MAIN ACTIVITIES

Body percussion

Children explore vibrations and sounds of their body instruments.

Challenge 1 (in pairs and whole class)

Musical buddies composition

Children work as 'musical buddies' to explore the range of their body instruments, including experimentation with body percussion sounds as part of a description of activities done in the natural world, e.g. rolling down a hill, splashing in a puddle or climbing a tree.

'Musical buddies' compose and rehearse a short sequence of body percussion sounds to perform in front of the rest of the class.

Extension activity (in pairs)

Children consider the dynamics of their composition, experimenting with the loudness and softness and the tempo (speed) of their body percussion sounds.

For further ideas on the development of body percussion, see the resources section.

Challenge 2 (in pairs)

Composition 'sound slide'

Children create a 'sound slide' to overlay natural objects, words, voice, movement and body percussion.

1. Working in pairs, the children collect natural materials/objects from the environment. They attribute a sound or sound word to each material/object.
2. Children lay their materials/objects out in a row. Each child stands on one side of the row of materials/objects, facing one another.
3. Children move in unison, sliding along the row of materials/objects, stopping at each and making the sound of the object through either body percussion or word, e.g. a piece of charcoal from the fire could be 'sizzle' (sound word), a rock could become 'stomp' (body percussion foot stomp), a stick could become 'snap' (body percussion finger click) or a length of wood or stick could become 'slide', which the children use to move along their sound slide, sounding it between each of the other materials/objects.
4. Children compose, rehearse then perform their sound slide to the rest of the class.

PLENARY

Discuss body percussion with the children. What have they learned about body percussion and how they can use their bodies to create sound in a performance? How did they use a 'sound slide' with natural objects? What did they learn about how natural objects can vibrate to create different sounds? Link to science by talking to the children about different materials producing different pitches: if an object vibrates quickly, we hear a high-pitched sound; if the same object vibrates slowly, we will hear a low-pitched sound. Sounds are made up of different kinds of sound waves.

EVALUATION/FOLLOW ON

- What went well today?
- Which children understood the concepts?
- Which children needed more help?
- Are there other resources you can use?
- Can the children develop their knowledge of sound back in the classroom?
- Can they carry out further investigations in sound?

PREPARATION

In advance of this session, set up six to ten 'sound points' in part of the outdoor area (see resources). Mark their locations on a map with a number.

These will be 'tune it in' stations. Children will visit each point to see whether they can name the sound, tune or instrument that is played by the items placed in sound boxes around the site. This sets the scene for the creation of the 'garden of sound'.

Resources

- Six to ten boxes containing musical instruments or items that make a sound

- Pictures and photographs of music walls, sound gardens and junk instruments.

- Resources for the sound garden will depend on what ideas the children have – see Challenges 1 and 2

- https://creativestarlearning. co.uk/c/art-music-outdoors

Previous learning

This reinforces listening skills from previous sessions and links to geography.

CONSIDER

Health & Safety

Assess and evaluate hazards and risks in your setting. See the health and safety chapter.

LESSON OBJECTIVES

We can work as part of a group and create a garden of sound, where a range of music dimensions can be experienced.

National Curriculum Content

- Improvise and compose music for a range of purposes, using the interrelated dimensions of music.

- Listen with attention to detail and recall sounds with increasing aural memory.

ADULT ROLES

- Support children to generate ideas

WARM UP IDEAS

Name that sound (groups of 4)

Place musical challenge stations (numbered) to 'name that sound' at varying locations in the outdoor environment, with a different sound at each point (see preparation and resources). Show the map (if being used).

Explain that at each musical challenge station there will be a box containing a sound or an item with which to make a sound.

Two of the children will create the sound and the other two children (blindfolded prior to the sound being made) will identify the sound.

They will need to record the number of the musical challenge station and write what they think the source of the sound is next to the number, e.g. it could be a musical instrument – a violin. It could be the clap of someone's hands or two saucepan lids banging together.

Introductory activity

Talk to the children about the sounds they have experienced in the outdoor area.

- Where are the best locations to create, hear and identify the sounds?

- Where is it most difficult to identify the sounds?

- If they were going to develop a 'garden of sound', where would they locate it?

MAIN ACTIVITIES

The garden of sound – it rocks!

Challenge 1 (whole class and groups of 4-6)
Creation of a garden of sound

Talk to the children about the creation of a garden of sound. This will be an area in which they can listen to and create a variety of sounds. It should include a performance area and a listening pod, where children can listen to a variety of music and sounds.

- The first thing the class will need to decide is whether there are any natural features in the environment where natural sounds can be created. Could this be a listening and composing zone?

- Look at examples of other sound areas in schools and gardens through pictures and images.

- The children then need to decide on what they are going to put into their sound garden. This could include a sound trail, a junk band area, a secret sound area, a listening pod and a stage area.

- Once the children have decided what they would like to include in the area, they will then need to be placed into working groups to develop each part of the garden of sound.

- The creation could take two or three outdoor learning sessions or it could be a simple creation completed within a session, depending on time.

Challenge 2 (groups of 4-6)
The big build

Working in small groups, children are given the opportunity to develop their part of the garden of sound. See the resources section for further ideas.

- Using the step-by-step principles for using tools, as identified in the health and safety chapter, children could develop a stage area using pallets, to be used in Progression 5 for the junk band.

- The stage could then be decorated with natural foliage.

- Musical notes could be made from willow; wooden discs decorated with different dynamic symbols could also be used to decorate the stage area.

- Other groups could develop a listening pod. This could be a shelter made with a tarpaulin or natural foliage, or willow transformed into a listening pod.

- An additional pod could be created as a composing pod.

- Show the children images of a music wall or a large xylophone and discuss how a music wall could be developed with a variety of junk items, such as pots and pans and beaters, or a large xylophone could be created using planks of wood.

- Sound boxes containing instruments or dynamics signature discs could be put in secret places.

- A 'sound trail' could be developed in order to enter the garden of sound.

Once the children have developed their part of the garden of sound, decide where each item will be placed if it was not built in location. How does the garden of sound work? Who will visit it? How will it change? Who will maintain it? Can a sound trail map be created to fully explore the garden of sound?

PLENARY

Talk to the children about how the garden of sound has been created. Has it covered all the elements of sound, such as dynamics? Are there a range of different sounds? Are there different pitches – high and low notes? Is the timbre rich? What do they still need to develop?

EVALUATION/FOLLOW ON

- What went well today?
- Which children understood the concepts?
- Which children needed more help?
- Are there other resources you can use?
- Can the children develop further sounds back in the classroom for the garden of sound?

PREPARATION

Prior to this session, show the children a clip from Stomp (see resources). This should inspire the children to think differently about junk and how it can be developed into music.

Resources

- Items of junk which could be used to make instruments, such as kitchen utensils, old containers, balloons, elastic bands, tubes or tape
- Stomp: www.youtube.com/watch?v=kdbuJkJsXt0
- www.thejunkorchestra.co.uk
- https://feltmagnet.com/crafts/Music-Instruments-for-Kids-to-Make
- Images of musical instruments made from junk
- Blindfolds
- Other resources or tools may be needed to make the children's planned junk instruments

CONSIDER

Health & Safety

Assess and evaluate hazards and risks in your setting. See the health and safety chapter.

Examples of instruments made from natural and artificial materials.

LESSON OBJECTIVES

We can create a musical composition with musical instruments made from junk and perform in a junk band.

National Curriculum Content

- Improvise and compose music for a range of purposes, using the interrelated dimensions of music.

ADULT ROLES

- Model the use of tools and how to make musical instruments from junk items
- Support the children in selecting materials and making junk instruments.

WARM UP IDEAS

Musical challenge: junk sounds and secret sounds (in pairs)

- One child will be blindfolded. The other child makes a secret sound. These can be made from voice, body percussion, natural materials/objects or using an item of junk from those previously collected.
- The child who is blindfolded has to guess what has made the sound. Each child is given three secret sound challenges and then they swap.
- Encourage the children to think about sound dynamics and how the sound can be made louder or softer. Use the wooden discs from Progression 2.
- Talk to the children about the different sounds they have created.
  - What sounds were most effective?
  - Which sounds were the easiest to guess?
  - Which sounds were harder?
  - Which sounds were more difficult to create dynamics with?

Introductory activity

Talk to the children about the clip they have seen from the musical Stomp. How have junk items been used to create musical instruments? Which instruments are simple to create and effective as instruments? Which instruments have they seen that they are most impressed by?

Ask the children to look at the junk items they have collected. Can they create a junk band as a class?

MAIN ACTIVITIES

The junk band

Challenge 1 (whole class and groups of 4-6)

Exploring sounds

Give the children the opportunity to experiment with the junk items to establish what sounds can be made.

- Show the children images of musical instruments made from junk.

- Talk to the children about the different sounds that will need to be created by a band.

- There will need to be some percussion instruments that create a beat (pulse).

- Some instruments will need to create a rhythm.

- Are there any instruments that can make a tune? What do we mean by the term 'tune'?

Once the children have explored the possible sound that can be created, place the children in groups (reflecting the sections of the orchestra).

- There could be a percussion group who are making shakers, drums, tambourines or similar creations.

- Another group could be a string group, using string, elastic bands and natural items to create instruments.

- There could be a group using only natural items to make instruments.

- One group could look at sounds using different amounts of water in jam jars.

- A 'pipes group' could create bagpipe-type instruments from clean, used hosepipes, or they can be whirled around (in a large space) using the air to create sound.

- Note: a tune can be created from an A4 slide clip used on files. Hum a tune into the clip and it can be heard through the clip.

- See the resources section of this progression for further ideas on making musical instruments from junk.

Once the groups have established their roles, give them the opportunity to make their instruments, using tools if required, following the principles in the health and safety chapter.

Challenge 2 (new groups of 4-6)

Composition – the junk band

Place the children in groups, with one child from each of the junk band creation groups forming a new group, i.e. each group will have someone from the strings group, percussion group, pipes group, etc., so that they have a range of instruments to make their band.

Encourage the children to develop a music composition using all the instruments in the band.

They create a musical piece or they could include a song.

Model some examples with a group using the instruments that have been made, remembering and demonstrating the dynamics of sound and the symbols they have used in previous sessions.

Do they need a conductor for their band to support them with the dynamics of their composition?

Performance and appreciation

Give the children the opportunity to perform their musical composition to other groups. Discuss and review each composition.

PLENARY

Which instruments have worked well? Which need further improvements? Which bands were most successful? What can we learn from other groups to support us further in the development of our junk band? How would you describe today's music? What did it make you think of? How did it make you feel?

EVALUATION/FOLLOW ON

- What went well today?

- Which children understood the concepts?

- Which children needed more help?

- Are there other resources you can use?

- Can the children develop their junk band further back in the classroom?

PREPARATION

Prior to this session, the children may wish to develop posters about their music festival and invite an audience to their performance. They may wish to dress in festival style.

Select items made in previous sessions that can be used in the performance, including musical instruments and songs the children have sung.

Prepare the garden of sound with a decorated stage.

Prepare an outline programme for the performance, in discussion with the children.

Resources

Resources will depend on the children's ideas.

- Resources and instruments from previous progressions as needed
- Items to decorate the stage
- Card and writing materials for making the programme

Previous learning

Children bring together all the learning from the past sessions as they perform in a music festival.

Examples of instruments made from natural materials.

LESSON OBJECTIVES

We can plan and perform in an outdoor music festival.

National Curriculum Content

- Improvise and compose music for a range of purposes, using the interrelated dimensions of music.
- Play and perform in solo and ensemble contexts, using their voices and playing musical instruments with increasing accuracy, fluency, control and expression.

ADULT ROLES

- Support the children in reflecting on their own performance and identifying areas where they can improve.

WARM UP IDEAS

Discuss with the children the variety of musical activities they have taken part in through the progressions of this unit. What have they most enjoyed about the sessions? What have they found the most difficult? What do they still need to work on prior to the music festival?

Introductory activity (in pairs)

Give the children the opportunity to reflect on the unit.

Ask them to discuss in pairs what they would like to do in the music festival.

- What would they like to perform?
- What instruments would they like to play?
- Who would they like to work with?

Give each pair a piece of card and ask them to write down their top three performance pieces. This can then be used to support the development of a programme in the next challenge.

CONSIDER

Health & Safety

Assess and evaluate hazards and risks in your setting. See the health and safety chapter.

Music festival – 'Music on the Wild Side'

Final rehearsal and performance of 'Music on the Wild Side' for performance as a musical ensemble.

Challenge 1 (individual, in pairs or groups of 4-6)
Planning the performance

In this challenge, children will need to decide on their performance and work as a solo, duet or small group to rehearse their performance.

In deciding what items will be in the performance, they will need to consider the following:

- What songs are they going to sing and where will this performance be located?
- How will they use the sound trail they have developed?
- At what point will the stage be used?
- Who will perform a body percussion piece of music?
- Which junk bands will perform?
- Can anyone play a musical instrument that could be used as part of the performance?
- Will the performance follow a theme or type of music?
- Are there a range of performances, including percussion, dynamics, part or whole orchestra and a conductor?

Once the programme for the music festival has been agreed, give the children the opportunity to rehearse their performances.

Talk to the children about what they are doing well, what they need to improve and how to prepare for the performance. What do they need to remember? What equipment do they need?

Challenge 2 (whole class)
Performance and appreciation

Give the children the opportunity to perform to an invited audience. This could be a class from the school or a local community group.

- Children could prepare posters and invitations in advance of the session.
- Refreshments that have been made by the children could be served.

Ensure that the children get the opportunity to appreciate the performances of their peers.

PLENARY

What part of the performance did the children most enjoy? Which parts do they think they performed well? Which parts could be improved? If they were to perform again, what would they change and why?

EVALUATION/FOLLOW ON

- What went well?
- Which children understood the concepts?
- Which children needed more help?
- Are there other resources you can use?
- Can the children develop their music further with the use of the junk band and the garden of sound?
- Can these areas be used to develop further curriculum links?
- Can the children write a review of the festival?
- Are there further opportunities to take part in music festivals in the local community?

Religious Education

Although a statutory 'basic curriculum' subject for all state-funded schools, religious education (RE) does not form part of the National Curriculum for England. However, this unit aims to support your local authority Standing Advisory Council on Religious Education (SACRE) statutory syllabus in the context of outdoor learning. The content of this unit reflects the aims of the non-statutory recommendations of the Religious Education Council of England and Wales (REC), 'A Curriculum Framework for Religious Education in England' (2013), published following the REC review and aiming to promote equity with other curriculum subjects. The REC suggest three main aims, for pupils to:

- A: Know about and understand a range of religions.

- B: Express ideas and insights about the nature, significance and impact of religions.

- C: Gain and deploy the skills needed to engage seriously with religions.

These are referenced as A, B and C in the attainment target aims within this unit. The activities also support the attainment targets (AT1 and AT2) of the 'Non-Statutory Framework for Religious Education' document (DCSF, 2010).

In this unit, children are encouraged to reflect and express meaning during enquiry-led experiential activities. They consider, observe and investigate possible answers to questions of identity, meaning and purpose, becoming detectives, looking for evidence in order to explore the nature of a possible god. They are encouraged to ask their own questions before giving reasons for their answers, and encouraged to go beyond expression of personal feelings or simple responses, in line with the English (spoken language) requirements. There are also links to Year 3 National Curriculum science (plants).

To support inclusive practice or to extend learning, the space, task, equipment and people (STEP) approach can be adopted throughout this unit. By changing the space, task, equipment or people, the activity can be made more challenging or easier to understand, enabling all pupils to take part in the activity, as explained in the assessment chapter in this book.

The children will be expected to work as a class directed by the teacher, together in small groups of two to four with support from adults, and independently. The role of the adult is to model and support the activities but also to allow time and space for the children to reflect on possible answers, to gather evidence, knowledge and understanding, and to draw conclusions or rethink initial ideas.

Natural connections

- Perceiving the unseen forces of nature
- Investigating seed dispersal
- Reflecting on the links between nature and religion.

Health and wellbeing

- Physical activity
- Expressing feelings
- Developing empathy
- Being calm and reflective.

Word bank

Religious terms

- God
- creator
- judge
- saviour
- Christian
- Holy Trinity
- Holy Spirit

- Allah
- Muslim
- Islamic
- pray
- rosary
- subha

Concepts

- unseen
- invisible
- mind's eye
- gravity
- love
- superpower
- perception
- metaphor
- detect
- clues

- evidence
- belief
- worldview
- reality
- meditation
- mindfulness
- affirmation
- tranquility
- nourish
- decade

Symbolism

- cross
- non-representational
- calligraphy

- tessellation
- geometric
- symmetrical

Summary overview

Progression	Curriculum content	Learning experiences/activities
Lesson 1	A: Describe, explain and analyse beliefs and practices, recognising the diversity that exists within and between communities and amongst individuals. B: Appreciate and appraise varied dimensions of religion or a worldview. C: Articulate beliefs, values and commitments clearly in order to explain why they may be important in their own and other people's lives.	Children explore ways of describing the concept of god and what it means to them and to others, if anything. They play 'I spy', creating pictures in the 'mind's eye' of others. They consider the answer to 'big questions', such as what is a god, where do our ideas of gods come from, what are gods in different religions like and why is it hard to describe the concept of god? They use imagery of natural objects in the area to describe their ideas about gods, reflecting on the power of words to create images in their 'mind's eye'.
Lesson 2	A: Describe, explain and analyse beliefs and practices, recognising the diversity that exists within and between communities and amongst individuals. B: Explain reasonably their ideas about how beliefs, practices and forms of expression influence individuals and communities.	Children explore ways of describing the concept of a god. They consider difficulties of believing in things that cannot be seen and how belief comes about through finding clues or evidence. Air currents, wind or bubbles are used as an example of this. They make a kite (with brief reference to the cross symbolism). They are guided to meditate and reflect on their learning by watching the seeds float in the wind.
Lesson 3	C: Find out about and investigate key concepts and questions of meaning, purpose and truth. Learning about religion (AT1): Identify religious beliefs and teachings in order to give a coherent account of a believer's response to the world. Learning from religion (AT2): Reflect upon questions of meaning and purpose. Identify and respond to values and commitments in themselves and others.	Children explore ways that Christians describe God. They encounter the Holy Trinity and its meaning in Christian beliefs. They explore the use of three to state three things that they are, before assembling a three-piece jigsaw from three leaves. They use sticks to make a 'Trinity Triangle'. Meditation through guided imagery is used.
Lesson 4		Children explore Muslim beliefs about Allah. A 'test the knot' activity is used prior to creating a 'circle of affirmation'. The children take turns to describe a classmate using only three to five words, using 'Step in'. They learn the 99 names for Allah and reflect on the power of the words and the meanings of the names.
Lesson 5		Children use 'Random pairing' and 'Walk and talk' to share their learning. The 99 names of Allah are revised, together with the fact that no images of Allah are allowed, with reasons discussed. They are introduced to Islamic art and creative calligraphy, and use natural materials to replicate these in the outdoor learning area.
Lesson 6		Children use 'Random pairing' and 'Walk and talk' to reflect on their learning. They identify leaves in the area, focusing on elder. They are introduced to subha and rosary prayer beads. They use elder wood to create beads, decorate and make decorative bead strings.

PREPARATION

Prepare a vocabulary list or cards of words that are commonly used to describe the concept of a god, such as creator, judge, saviour, scary, loving, kind, not real, everywhere, etc.

Resources

- Selection of dried leaves (or cards)
- Marker pens
- Vocabulary cards

CONSIDER

Health & Safety

Assess and evaluate hazards and risks in your setting. See the health and safety chapter.

LESSON OBJECTIVES

We are learning to explain our understanding of unseen things and to describe our understanding of gods in general and of the Christian God.

Attainment targets

A Describe, explain and analyse beliefs and practices, recognising the diversity that exists within and between communities and amongst individuals.

B Appreciate and appraise varied dimensions of religion or a worldview.

C Articulate beliefs, values and commitments clearly in order to explain why they may be important in their own and other people's lives.

ADULT ROLES

- Allow time for children to process the questions, reflect, gather information, clarify or verify using partner talk, and draw conclusions, before asking them to give justified answers.

- Record the children's metaphors, using voice recorders, video or photographs.

WARM UP IDEAS

Explain that for the next six sessions the children will thinking about how God is described in different world religions: Christianity and Islam.

Introductory activity (whole class and in pairs)

I spy

1. Teacher describes something they can see, aiming to create images in the children's 'mind's eye', and the children guess at what it could be.
   - Did the children see things in their 'mind's eye'? Did they all guess the same thing?
   - Do they think they saw the same 'mind's eye' image as their friend?
   - Explain that sometimes, even though they may have the same information, people see things in different ways and this can help explain how some people believe or understand things differently.

2. Pairs take it in turns to describe something from the area that they can see, adding detail using appropriate adjectives. Can they describe it so exactly that their partner knows what it is without too many guesses?

3. Ask the children 'How can we describe something that is there, but that we cannot see?' or 'What can we sense but not see?', such as gravity, heat, love, the wind. How do we know it is there? Explain that not everything that 'is' can be seen. With a partner, try to describe the wind.

MAIN ACTIVITIES

Unseen god

Challenge 1 (whole class and in pairs)

Answer questions and deliberate on possible answers

1. What is a god?

Ask 'What is a god?' (A being thought to have power to control the world or aspects of it.)

What experience or knowledge of a god do they have, if any? Discuss with a talking partner.

The children tell a talking partner what they think a god does and what they might be like, prompted by the vocabulary cards..

The children's ideas may come from family beliefs, stories, collective worship at school, experience of being part of a religious community or less conventional sources such as films and computer games. They might attribute god-like qualities to a variety of different beings, such as having a superpower or being 'super-knowledgeable' or having 'super-perception', which is how a god might know what you are doing!

2. Where do our ideas about gods come from?

Ask 'Where do our ideas about gods come from?'

Acknowledge that some people believe in a god and some don't.

What religions can they remember? Do all religions have a god? What do they already know?

3. What is the Christian God like?

Today we are looking at the Christian understanding of God – 'What is the Christian God like?'

Use the model: 'I think the Christian God is... ', e.g. 'I think the Christian God is a judge' or 'I think the Christian God is loving', etc.

Using marker pens, ask the children to write their descriptions onto leaves or cards cut into the shape of leaves, or simply discuss through partner talk.

4. Why is it hard to describe the Christian God?

They may give answers such as 'God can't be seen', etc., bringing them back to the wind. Does that mean that God does not exist? Compare God to the wind; they know it's there, but they can't see it.

One way we explain difficult things is by the use of imagery.

Challenge 2 (whole class and in pairs)

Use natural objects to describe ideas about god using imagery

Explain that imagery is often used to explain difficult things and make them clearer. Give one or two examples using natural objects found in the learning area, e.g. 'If God was a leaf, God would be golden, perfect and have no marks' or 'If God was a tree, God would be stretching right up to the sky', etc.

Scaffold the sentence by providing a verbal template: 'If God was a... , God would be... '

Other ideas could include plants, flowers, animals, colours, etc., according to the setting.

In pairs, walk around the area comparing what they see to their idea about god.

PLENARY

Encourage the children to explain what they have been doing in the session and state what they have found out about what people in the class think about the idea of god. Does everyone think the same things? Summarise for the class what the metaphors say about ideas of god. Are images created in their 'mind's eye' or through metaphor an easier way to see things described by others? Is it better to represent someone or something using words or pictures? (This point will be revisited in Progression 4.)

EVALUATION/FOLLOW ON

- What went well and why?
- What didn't go as well as expected?
- What could be changed?
- Who stood out and why?

PREPARATION

Source suitable 'helicopter' seeds and sticks and twigs for the kites and scatter them in the learning area, if they are not already present.

Resources

- Two straight sticks per child

- Bin bags, lengths of string, scissors and colourful ribbon for kite tails

- Sycamore, field maple or ash tree seeds ('helicopter' seeds) – if you don't have these, use bubbles instead as explained in the Warm up ideas

Previous learning

This progression extends understanding of 'believing in things that cannot be seen' from Progression 1.

It links to Year 3 science (plants) attainment targets.

CONSIDER

Health & Safety

Assess and evaluate hazards and risks in your setting. See the health and safety chapter.

LESSON OBJECTIVES

We are exploring how we know things exist.

Attainment targets

A Describe, explain and analyse beliefs and practices, recognising the diversity that exists within and between communities and amongst individuals.

B Explain reasonably their ideas about how beliefs, practices and forms of expression influence individuals and communities.

C Find out about and investigate key concepts and questions of meaning, purpose and truth.

ADULT ROLES

- Encourage the children to see the relevance and importance of the questions that are being asked and how they relate to them.

- Allow time for children to process the questions, reflect, gather information, clarify or verify using partner talk, and to draw conclusions, before asking them to give justified answers.

- Model the activity, acknowledging challenges and sharing possible solutions.

- Assist with tying the knots of the kite.

WARM UP IDEAS

Ask the children to share with a talking partner their ideas, descriptions and beliefs about what they think a god is, does and the effect that belief in a god has on people's lives.

Introductory activity (in pairs and whole class)

Remind the children about believing in things that cannot be seen and why belief sometimes comes about through finding clues or evidence.

Revisit the discussions about gravity and the wind from Progression 1 – how they cannot be seen but are there, as we can feel them and see their effects.

Make links to Year 3 science (plants – seed dispersal) by exploring 'helicopter seeds' from sycamore, field maple or ash trees, demonstrating how the seeds fly and spin through the air.

Ask the children to explain what stops them falling to the ground immediately and why they travel. How is the 'helicopter' effect created?

If seeds are not available, then use bubbles to show the effect of air currents. Discuss:

- Can we see the effect that gravity, wind and moving air has on trees and plants?

- Big question: Can we explain the existence of things we cannot see or do we just have to believe that they are there? How do we know? Are there always clues?

- We can use other senses to know things exist.

MAIN ACTIVITIES

Invisible and real

Emphasise the point that just because we can't see things, it doesn't mean they are not there – but we can see the effect they might have, e.g. what could we do on a windy day to use the effect of the invisible wind? If it is windy, go fly kites! Let's use kites to show the evidence of the wind.

Challenge 1 (in pairs and whole class)

Make a kite using sticks and a bin bag

1. In pairs, find two straight, slender sticks, one shorter than the other.
2. Model how to make the kite frame by crossing the shorter stick (cross spar) about one third of the way down the main stick (spine).
3. What does this make? Brief links to Christian symbolism can be made here, by asking what the cross represents and why it is important to Christians.
4. Use square lashing with string to fix the two sticks together.
5. Cut the bin bag (sail) to fit the frame of the kite and tie the corners of the bin bag to the four ends of the stick frame using the string.
6. Create a 'bridle' by tying string from the middle of each side of the cross spar, leaving enough slack to form a triangle when gently pulled (vertex).
7. Attach a kite line to the bottom of the main stick and also to the vertex of the bridle, tying a simple knot where the strings cross so that it forms a triangular pyramid.
8. Tie ribbon to the bottom of the spine to help balance it (add light twigs for extra weight).
9. With a partner, launch the kite and spend some time keeping the kites flying, repairing or improving them where necessary.

Note: If time is short, simply attach strings to the handles of a plastic carrier bag and fly it.

Challenge 2 (whole class)

How do we show our understanding or belief in things that cannot be seen?

Re-emphasise the point that just because we can't see things, it doesn't mean that they are not there – but we can see the effect they might have.

Introduce a 'worldview' that 'reality' isn't only what we can see and touch (the physical world) – that we can't determine what is real simply by what we can immediately detect with our senses (sight, smell, touch, hearing and taste).

Challenge 3 (whole class)

How does flying a kite relate to finding evidence of a god?

To find out whether something is real, we need to look for evidence or clues, such as the wind keeping the kites up, or moving the trees and seeds, or moving the bubbles.

- What evidence could they use, for example, to prove that a god is the creator of the universe?
- Can they make a case for the existence of a god, e.g. that nature is so complex that it must have been created? Can they make a case for there not being a god, e.g. scientists can explain how the world works and how it began?

PLENARY

Use the falling seeds to lead the children towards breathing meditation, guided imagery and mindfulness, by encouraging them to watch the seeds move in the air. As they watch, ask them to listen to their breathing, slow their breathing down and to contemplate:

- What have they learned about believing in things that cannot be seen?
- What have they learned about being a detective?
- What have they learned about working with a partner and teamwork?

Back in the classroom

The seeds can be taken back into class and used to make natural art, such as dragonflies (using twigs as the body and painted in iridescent paint or diluted poster paints) or birds and flowers. Or the children could use them to express in art what ideas of a god means to them.

EVALUATION/FOLLOW ON

- What went well and why?
- What didn't go as well as expected?
- What could be changed?
- Who stood out and why?

PREPARATION

Collect large leaves and cut them into three pieces.

Place three sets of jigsaw leaves in separate envelopes, one for each group, or, if on site, the leaves can be simply placed on separate tree stumps.

Peel the bark from two sticks and keep another one unpeeled to model Challenge 1.

Resources

- Selection of large leaves cut into three pieces, sufficient for three leaf jigsaws per group
- Leaf identification guide
- Selection of sticks from the area or ice lolly sticks
- Knives or peelers to strip the bark and safety gloves
- Permanent markers
- String or pipe cleaners
- Scissors

CONSIDER

Health & Safety

Assess and evaluate hazards and risks in your setting. See the health and safety chapter.

LESSON OBJECTIVES

We are learning about the nature of God in Christianity, as represented by the Holy Trinity.

Attainment targets

A   Describe, explain and analyse beliefs and practices, recognising the diversity that exists within and between communities and amongst individuals.

B   Explain reasonably their ideas about how beliefs, practices and forms of expression influence individuals and communities.

C   Find out about and investigate key concepts and questions of meaning, purpose and truth.

ADULT ROLES

- Allow time for children to process the questions, reflect, gather information, clarify or verify using partner talk, and draw conclusions, before asking them to give justified answers.
- Model the activity, acknowledging challenges and sharing possible solutions.

WARM UP IDEAS

Explain that this session is continuing our understanding of the nature of God as described by Christians. Today we will be learning about the Holy Trinity. Explain that 'tri' means three. What other words can they think of that use 'tri'?

Tell them three things that you are, such as an aunt (uncle), a mother (father) and a sister (brother).

In pairs, state **three** things about themselves that describe what they are, e.g. 'I am a son, a brother and a netball player'.

Introductory activity (groups of four to six)

Leaf jigsaw

Supply groups with the three sets of three-piece jigsaw leaves and the leaf identification sheet. Say that there are three whole leaves that have been cut into three parts. They have three minutes to put the leaves back together and to identify them using the identification card.

When the time is up, see which groups have succeeded in the challenge.

- How well did the team work? Did anyone stand out as a good leader? Why was this?
- What did the children use to help them match the leaves?
- What are the types of leaf that they have as their jigsaw? Are they sure?
- What are the identifying features, e.g. colour, jagged edges, round or heart-shaped, etc.?

MAIN ACTIVITIES

Holy Trinity

The children have been exploring elements using three in the lesson. Reintroduce the word 'Trinity' and clarify that it means a group of three or representing three things. Explain that Christians believe that God is a Trinity. Although Christians believe in only one God, he is known as God the Father, God the Son and God the Holy Spirit, just as they learned that they themselves could be three things in the warm up activity.

Clarify that it is not three Gods, nor three people joined to make one God; it is one God in three states. A comparison could be made to water being vapour, liquid and solid. It's still water. Acknowledge that it is very confusing and that even some Christians don't understand it properly.

Explain that Christians use the phrase 'the Father, the Son, and the Holy Spirit' as a way of describing God.

Challenge 1 (whole class)

How to use sticks to represent the Trinity

Show the children your three prepared sticks. Explain that each stick will represent part of the Trinity.

1. Show how to use the knife or peeler to safely strip or peel the bark from a stick, leaving the pale inner wood, which can now be decorated.
2. On one stick, write 'Father'; on another, 'Son'; and on the third, 'Holy Spirit'.
3. Explain that each stick could also be decorated
4. The sticks could be decorated using colourful pipe cleaners wound around the stick, threaded with beads or using leaves and found objects from the learning area.

5. Show how to lash the sticks together at the ends using string or wired raffia to create a triangle and how to use a shorter piece of string for hanging the 'Trinity Triangle' up.

Note: If not using tools, use lolly sticks or pre-peeled sticks.

Challenge 2 (individual)

Make their own 'Trinity Triangles'

The children follow the steps demonstrated above to make their own 'Trinity Triangles'.

PLENARY

Share the 'Trinity Triangles'. Encourage the children to explain what they have been doing in the lesson and state what new things they have learned.

Lead the children towards breathing meditation, guided imagery and mindfulness, by encouraging them to listen to sounds in the area, watch leaves on the trees moving against the sky or gaze at their 'Trinity Triangle'. As they listen or watch, ask them to slow their breathing, to listen to their breathing and to contemplate the learning today. Guide them to think about the different emotions they may feel – sometimes happy, sometimes sad, sometimes tired, sometimes bored, sometimes excited, etc. No matter how they feel, they are still the same person.

EVALUATION/FOLLOW ON

- What went well and why?
- What didn't go as well as expected?
- What could be changed?
- Who stood out and why?
- Can they describe what the Trinity means for Christians?
- Can they name the three parts of the Trinity?

PREPARATION

Source a list of the 99 names of Allah and write some of them on cards or leaves.

Resources

- 13 m length of tubular webbing (or sets of 6 m lengths if using smaller groups)
- Cards or leaves with some of the 99 names of Allah written on them

Previous learning

This session links to Raccoon Circles in Year 3 maths progressions and Progression 2 in this set.

CONSIDER

Health & Safety

Assess and evaluate hazards and risks in your setting. See the health and safety chapter.

LESSON OBJECTIVES

We are exploring Muslim beliefs about the nature of God (Allah) and Allah's 99 names.

Attainment targets

A Describe, explain and analyse beliefs and practices, recognising the diversity that exists within and between communities and amongst individuals.

B Explain reasonably their ideas about how beliefs, practices and forms of expression influence individuals and communities.

C Find out about and investigate key concepts and questions of meaning, purpose and truth.

ADULT ROLES

- Allow time for children to process the questions, reflect, gather information, clarify or verify using partner talk, and draw conclusions, before asking them to give justified answers.
- Model the activity, acknowledging challenges and sharing possible solutions.

WARM UP IDEAS

Explain that the children will be learning about Muslim beliefs about the concept of god. Remind the children about how they described the Christian God using words (metaphors). Did they find it difficult? Why was that? Can words clearly show another person what you are trying to describe? Or was it easier or clearer to create pictures in the mind's eye? Can they follow instructions that are just spoken?

Introductory activity (whole class or groups of eight)

Test the knot

Join the ends of the 13 m tubular webbing using a water knot.

1. The children stand in a circle holding the webbing 'overhand' (over the top of the tape, rather than grabbing it from below) at waist height.
2. Ensure that the children are well spaced and that they are all exerting the same amount of pressure on the webbing. This may take a bit of practice!
3. Maintaining the pressure on the webbing, ask the children to slowly lean back slightly and bend their knees.
4. They bend their knees a bit more, gradually lowering their bottoms to the ground, without falling over.
5. Ensure safe practice, but do allow the children to have a few goes.
6. Can they feel how the person next to them supports them? Can they feel the whole team working together to support one another? Do they do this in the classroom? How does this make them feel?

Note: This can also be done using in groups of eight using shorter lengths of webbing, e.g. 6 m lengths, which could add an element of competition.

MAIN ACTIVITIES

Allah's 99 names

Using the circle of tubular webbing from the introductory activity, place the webbing on the ground to make a perfect circle. This may take some practice. Explain that the circle now represents the 'circle of affirmation'!

Challenge 1 (whole class)
The circle of affirmation and 'Step in'

With the children standing around the outside of the circle, remind them about describing a god in Progression 1. They are going to develop these ideas by thinking of words that describe one of their classmates.

1. Ask the children to think of three to five words to share that could be used to describe one of their friends in the class.
2. To provide thinking and processing time to find the three to five appropriate words, walk the children once around the outside of the circle, stopping once they have returned to their original places. This may also take a bit of practice.
3. Ask for one volunteer to 'step in' to the circle to describe their classmate. You may like to choose this volunteer carefully, as they will provide a model for the challenge. You may prefer them to whisper the words to you first or to model the activity yourself.
4. As they describe their classmate in three to five words, make sure they do not look at the classmate they are describing. Can the class guess who is being described?
5. The volunteer decides who will step into the circle, by choosing one child to 'affirm their answers' by stepping into the circle, stating their guess then stepping out of the circle again. If the answer is incorrect, another child is chosen to step into the circle and guess. If they are correct they become the volunteer.
6. Repeat the activity.
7. Ask the children to assess how hard it was to guess the classmate being described using only a few words. Easy? Hard?

Challenge 2 (whole class)
Assessing using webbing circle as the gauge

1. Ask the children to pick up the webbing, maintaining the circle shape.
2. Ask them to show how hard they thought Challenge 1 was to achieve, using the webbing as a gauge. Holding the webbing up high means that it was easy; holding it down low means that they found it difficult.
3. The children show how they feel using the webbing gauge. By keeping the webbing under tension in this way, they will feel pressure from people either side of them. Can they feel the support or tension from others who found it less or more difficult?

Challenge 3 (whole class)
Reflection on the 99 names of Allah

Place the webbing on the ground in a circle.

1. Explain that Muslims call their god Allah, and believe that it is wrong to represent Allah using pictures or images, and therefore use words as opposed to images to describe Allah.
2. Did they know that there are 99 names describing Allah? Give a few examples.
3. Give each child a card or leaf describing Allah.
4. One at a time, the children 'step in' to read their card (with adult support where needed).
5. After clarifying the meanings of any unknown vocabulary, allow time to think about how the descriptions make them feel.
6. Ask the children to reflect on how the names show us what Muslims think about Allah.

PLENARY

Magic spot reflection

Ask the children find a space by themselves to sit quietly under a tree or in a bush to find some quiet time. Ask them to consider what they have been doing in the session and what powerful words they could use to state what they have found out about Muslim beliefs.

Regroup and share some of their thoughts.

EVALUATION/FOLLOW ON

- What went well and why?
- What didn't go as well as expected?
- What could be changed?
- Who stood out and why?

PREPARATION

Resources

- 13 m length of tubular webbing
- Collection of sticks and natural objects
- Images of Islamic artwork

Previous learning

Discuss different joining techniques, favourite structures and designs and new ideas.

CONSIDER

Health & Safety

Assess and evaluate hazards and risks in your setting. See the health and safety chapter.

LESSON OBJECTIVES

We are exploring Muslim beliefs about the nature of Allah and how non-representational artwork can reflect Muslim understanding about Allah.

Attainment targets

A Describe, explain and analyse beliefs and practices, recognising the diversity that exists within and between communities and amongst individuals.

B Explain reasonably their ideas about how beliefs, practices and forms of expression influence individuals and communities.

C Find out about and investigate key concepts and questions of meaning, purpose and truth.

ADULT ROLES

- Allow time for children to process the questions, reflect, gather information, clarify or verify using partner talk, and draw conclusions, before asking them to give justified answers.

- Model the activity, acknowledging challenges and sharing possible solutions.

WARM UP IDEAS

Revise the previous lesson about Muslim beliefs about Allah and the 99 names of Allah using 'Walk and talk'.

Introductory activity (whole class and in pairs)

'Random pairing' and 'Walk and talk'

This is a great way to give the children the chance to interact with children outside of their immediate friendship group. You can also assess learning by listening to the conversations!

1. Holding the webbing at waist height, the class make a circle.
2. Carefully work together to place it on the ground. This may take a few attempts – remedy any problems as they occur.
3. Every other child steps into the circle so that an equal number of children are outside and inside the circle. 'Insiders' turn to the right and 'outsiders' turn to the left.
4. On your signal, the insiders and outsiders walk around the circle in opposite directions, i.e. the insiders anticlockwise and the outsiders clockwise.
5. Once the children have walked around the circle for a bit, call out 'Stop!' and the children turn to face the person nearest to them – an outsider facing an insider.
6. This is now their talking and sharing partner to share ideas and talk through answers.
7. The children stand shoulder to shoulder in their relative positions (with tubular webbing between them on the ground) and all walk in the same direction, e.g. clockwise.
8. As they walk, they talk, with the insider as listener and outsider as talker.
9. Ask the children to share what they have learned so far about Muslim beliefs about Allah. What names can they remember? What were their favourite names? How did the names make them feel? Why are there no images of Allah?
10. The children swap places and roles at the knot.

MAIN ACTIVITIES

Islamic art

Briefly remind the children that Muslims represent Allah with words, e.g. the Peace, the Tranquillity, the Nourisher and the Designer, and ask the children for possible reasons for this. For example:

• Any picture of Allah would only be that artist's view.

• They might worship the picture rather than Allah.

• If there are different 'aspects' of Allah, how could a picture reflect that?

Explain that although Muslims do not believe it is right to draw or make images of Allah, they do use calligraphy (special writing) and create beautiful non-representational artwork, often using colours to represent different aspects of Allah.

Challenge 1 (whole class and individual)

Create non-representational artwork using natural materials

Show the children the Islamic art images. Discuss the symmetry, tessellations, patterns, geometric shapes and colour, linking to the maths progressions.

1. Model how to choose a name, then create patterns and shapes using stones, gravel, sticks, leaves, earth, grasses, etc. from the area, adding colour too.

2. Independently, the children choose a name that inspires them and use this to create patterns as modelled, using sticks, etc.

Challenge 2 (whole class and individual)

Experiment with line and calligraphy patterns using natural materials

1. Show the children images of numbers or letters represented by calligraphy.

2. Model how to use mud and earth (or chalks) to draw lines on the ground or appropriate surfaces.

3. Encourage the children to create their own calligraphic designs. These can represent numbers or their names.

PLENARY

Encourage the children to explain what they have been doing in the session and state what they have found out about.

Back in the classroom

The children do a short piece of writing to describe how the name they chose inspired them in their work.

EVALUATION/FOLLOW ON

• What went well and why?

• What didn't go as well as expected?

• What could be changed?

• Who stood out and why?

PREPARATION

Ensure that the area to be used has been checked for hazards.

If tools are not to be used, pre-cut the elder sticks.

If you have time, make an example bracelet out of elder – see Challenge 1.

Resources

- Leaf identification sheets, e.g. the Leaf Spotter guide from the Woodland Trust website
- Elder leaves and elder sticks
- Coloured marker pens
- String or coloured wool
- Optional: secateurs or loppers, knives or peelers, hacksaws and safety gloves

CONSIDER

Health & Safety

Assess and evaluate hazards and risks in your setting. See the health and safety chapter.

LESSON OBJECTIVES

We are making prayer and meditation beads and using them to reflect on our learning.

Attainment targets

A   Describe, explain and analyse beliefs and practices, recognising the diversity that exists within and between communities and amongst individuals.

B   Explain reasonably their ideas about how beliefs, practices and forms of expression influence individuals and communities.

C   Find out about and investigate key concepts and questions of meaning, purpose and truth.

ADULT ROLES

- Allow time for children to process the questions, reflect, gather information, clarify or verify using partner talk, and draw conclusions, before asking them to give justified answers.
- Model the activity, acknowledging challenges and sharing possible solutions.

WARM UP IDEAS

Revise the previous sessions using 'Random pairing' and 'Walk and talk', as in Progression 5.

Ask the children to share with their talking partner what they have learned so far about Christian and Muslim beliefs. Can they identify one or two things that have been most memorable or meaningful? Ask them to give reasons for their choice, reassuring them that it is OK to rethink their initial ideas in the light of new knowledge and understanding.

Introductory activity

1. Hand out the leaf identification sheet and ask the children to identify the different features of the leaves on the sheet by shape or descriptions, such as jagged, smooth or symmetrical.
2. Introduce (or revise) terms such as simple (single leaves such as beech) or compound (two or more parts to the leaf, such as elder) and encourage the children to use the vocabulary.
3. Can they identify the difference between elder, ash and rowan leaves?
4. Show them an elder leaf and identify the key features of the leaf.
5. Using the leaf they have been given as a guide, ask them to find elder trees in the learning area, if available. Look at the shape of the tree and for any berries that may remain on the tree.
6. If no elders are available, then use the identification sheet to identify other trees in the setting.

MAIN ACTIVITIES

Meditation beads

Gather the children and again show the example of an elder bead string or the subha and rosary bead strings. Explain that some Muslims and Christians use bead threads to help them to meditate and pray.

How many names for Allah are there? Explain that Muslims use prayer beads with 99 beads on them. As the beads are passed through the fingers, they recite the names of Allah or say special prayers.

Explain that some Christians also have prayer beads called rosary beads, and show an example if possible. The 108 beads in a rosary, arranged in five groups of ten beads called a 'decade', are each separated by a slightly larger bead, used to count and keep track of prayers.

Tell the children that today's challenge will be to make their own necklace or bracelet. It won't be used for prayers or have religious significance.

Challenge 1 (whole class)

How to make an elder bead string

Model how to make elder beads.

1. Choose and cut a long straight stick from the elder tree, about the thickness of a finger, using secateurs or loppers. Try to find 'green' wood if possible.

2. Demonstrate how to safely strip off the bark using a knife or potato peeler, peeling away from the body. This can also be used to make patterns on the bark, such as stripes.

3. Cut the stick into bead-sized lengths (about 3cm) using a hacksaw. Ask one child to hold the stick steady, hands well apart, while the wood is being sawn. Safety gloves should be worn.

4. Show the children how the core of the elder is soft and pushes out quite easily. A skewer or a tent peg can be used to do this, always pushing away from the body.

5. This hollow tube is the bead and can now be decorated using permanent marker pens.

6. Show how to thread the beads onto the string.

Challenge 2 (in pairs or groups of four)

Make their own bead strings

The children source slender branches and follow the modelled instructions.

How many beads can they make? Will the beads all be the same size? What colours will they choose and what significance will the colours have?

Emphasise that these are bracelets and necklaces and have no religious significance.

PLENARY

Ask the children to come up with explanations of what they have been doing in the sessions and share these with a partner or in small groups.

Back in the classroom

In computing, the children find photographs of rosary or subha beads. They add text boxes or speech bubbles to explain the purpose of the beads.

EVALUATION/FOLLOW ON

- What went well and why?
- What didn't go as well as expected?
- What could be changed?
- Who stood out and why?

Key resources for Year 3 progressions

Brocklehurst, R. (2013) *The Victorians* (Usborne History of Britain). London: Usborne Publishing.

Corbett, P. & Moses, B. (1986) *Catapults and Kingfishers*. Oxford: Oxford University Press.

Flint, I. (2008) *Eco Colour: Botanical Dyes for Beautiful Textiles*. Sydney, Australia: Murdoch Books.

Goodman, R. (2013) *How to be a Victorian*. London: Viking Publishing.

Hughes, E. (2015) *The Little Gardener*. London: Flying Eye Books.

Irvine, R. (2019) *Forest Craft*. Lewes: GMC Publications.

Mabey, R. (2012) *Food for Free*. London: Collins.

McDonnell, P. (2011) *Me...Jane*. New York: Little, Brown & Company.

O'Neill, M. (1999) *Hailstones and Halibut Bones*. New York: Doubleday Books.

Potter, B. (2002) *The Complete Tales*, London: Frederick Warne.

Potter, B. (2006) *A Journal*. London: Frederick Warne.

Rawlinson, J. (2006) *Fletcher and the Falling Leaves*. New York: HarperCollins Publishers.

Sidman, J. (2010) *Dark Emperor and Other Poems of the Night*. Boston, MASS: Houghton Mifflin Books for Children.

Bibliography

Araneda, D., Guzmán, M.A. & Nussbaum, M. (2019) The national curriculum vs. the ideal curriculum: acknowledging student learning interests, *Oxford Review of Education*, 45 (3), 333-349.

Aronsson, J., Waite, S. & Tighe Clark, M. (2015) Measuring the impact of outdoor learning on the physical activity of school age children: The use of accelerometry. *Education and Health*, 33 (3). Available online at: http://sheu.org.uk/sheux/EH/eh333ja.pdf.

Atjonen, P. (2014) Teachers' views of their assessment practice. *The Curriculum Journal*, 25 (2), 238-259.

Ball, D., Gill, T. & Spiegal, B. (2008) Managing Risk in Play Provision: Implementation guide. Nottingham, England: National Children's Bureau and Play England. Available online at: http://www.playengland.org.uk/media/172644/managing-risk-in-play-provision.pdf

Bølling, M., Otte, C., Elsborg, P., Nielson, G. & Bentsen, P. (2018) The association between education outside the classroom and students' school motivation: Results from a one-school-year quasi-experiment. *International Journal of Educational Research*. 89, 22-35.

Bourn, D., Hunt, F., Blum, N. & Lawson, H. (2016) Primary education for global learning and sustainability. Report for Cambridge Primary Review. Available online at: https://cprtrust.org.uk/wp-content/uploads/2016/02/Bourn-report-160217-final.pdf.

British Orienteering (no date) Tri-O: Orienteering made easy. Available online at: www.britishorienteering.org.uk/images/uploaded/downloads/schools_tri_o_resources.pdf.

Cain, J. & Smith, T. (2007) *The Revised and Expanded Book of Raccoon Circles*. Dubuque, Iowa: Kendall Hunt publishing.

Cornell, J. (1999) *Sharing Nature with Children*. Nevada City: Dawn Publications.

Cornwall Agreed Syllabus for Religious Education (2014). Available online at: https://www.cornwall.gov.uk/media/9227047/Agreed-syllabus-2014.pdf.

Danks, F. & Schofield, J. (2010) *Make it Wild!: 101 Things to Make and Do Outdoors*. London: Frances Lincoln Publishers Ltd.

Department for Children, Schools and Families (DCSF) (2010) Religious education in English schools: Non-statutory guidance. Available online at: https://assets.publishing.service.gov.uk/government/uploads/system/uploads/attachment_data/file/190260/DCSF-00114-2010.pdf.

Department for Education (DfE) (2014) National Curriculum in England: Framework for Key Stages 1 to 4. Available online at: www.gov.uk/government/collections/national-curriculum.

Department for Education (DfE) (2018a) Health and safety: responsibilities and duties for schools. Available online at: https://www.gov.uk/government/publications/health-and-safety-advice-for-schools/responsibilities-and-duties-for-schools.

Department for Education (DfE) (2018b) Mental health and behaviour in schools. Available online at: https://assets.publishing.service.gov.uk/government/uploads/system/uploads/attachment_data/file/755135/Mental_health_and_behaviour_in_schools__.pdf.

Department for Environment, Food and Rural Affairs (DEFRA) (2018) A Green Future: Our 25 Year Plan to Improve the Environment. Available online at: https://assets.publishing.service.gov.uk/government/uploads/system/uploads/attachment_data/file/693158/25-year-environment-plan.pdf.

Department of Health and Social Care (DHSC) (2018) Prevention is better than cure: Our vision to help you live well for longer. Available online at: https://assets.publishing.service.gov.uk/government/uploads/system/uploads/attachment_data/file/753688/Prevention_is_better_than_cure_5-11.pdf.

Dweck, C. (2007) *Mindset: The new psychology of success*. New York: Ballantine Books.

Educational Endowment Foundation (2018) Metacognition and Self-regulated Learning. Available online at: https://educationendowmentfoundation.org.uk/tools/guidance-reports/metacognition-and-self-regulated-learning.

Edwards-Jones, A., Waite, S. & Passy, R. (2018) Falling into LINE: School strategies for overcoming challenges associated with learning in natural environments (LINE), *Education 3–13*, 46 (1), 49–63.

Garrick, R. (2009) *Playing Outdoors in the Early Years*. London: Continuum.

Gill, T. (2016) Balancing Benefits and Risks in Outdoor Learning and Play. Available online at: https://outdoorclassroomday.org.uk/wp-content/uploads/sites/2/2016/06/160606_PROJECTDIRT_ECD_BOOK7_A4-1.pdf.

Green, M. & Somerville, M. (2015) Sustainability education: Researching practice in primary schools, *Environmental Education Research*, 21 (6), 832–845.

Hammett, E. (2016) Fulfilling the first aid requirements in schools. *British Journal of School Nursing*, 11 (7), 1–4. Available online at: https://firstaidforlife.org.uk/wp-content/uploads/2017/03/BJSN-Schools-First-Aid-Sept-2016-2.pdf

Hawe, E. & Parr, J. (2014). Assessment for Learning in the writing classroom: an incomplete realisation. *The Curriculum Journal*, 25 (2), 210–237.

Health and Safety Executive (HSE) (2018) How do the Health and Safety (First-Aid) Regulations 1981 relate to first-aid provision in schools? Available online at: www.hse.gov.uk/firstaid

Ho, S. (2014) The purposes outdoor education does, could and should serve in Singapore. *Journal of Adventure Education and Outdoor Learning*, 14 (2), 153–171.

Hopper, R. (2017) Special educational needs and disability and learning outside the classroom. In: Waite, S. (ed.) *Children Learning Outside the Classroom: From Birth to Eleven (2nd edition)*. London: SAGE, pp. 118–130.

Hunt, A., Stewart, D., Richardson, M., Hinds J., Bragg, R., White, M. & Burt, J. (2017) Monitor of Engagement with the Natural Environment: developing a method to measure nature connection across the English population (adults and children). Natural England Commissioned Reports, Number 233. York: Natural England.

Institute for Outdoor Learning (2018) Teaching outdoors. Available online at: www.outdoor-learning.org/Good-Practice/Develop-your-Organisation/Outdoor-Learning-in-Schools/Teaching-Outdoors.

Lambert, D. (2014) *Taking Maths Outdoors with Raccoon Circles*. Available from Taking Maths Outdoors Facebook page.

Council for Learning Outside the Classroom (CLOtC) (2018) Get ready – managing risk. Available online at: www.lotc.org.uk/plan-deliver-lotc/planning-lotc-experiences/get-ready-managing-risk.

Malone, K. & Waite, S. (2016) Student Outcomes and Natural Schooling: Pathways from Evidence to Impact Report 2016. Available online at: https://www.plymouth.ac.uk/uploads/production/document/path/6/6811/Student_outcomes_and__natural_schooling_pathways_to_impact_2016.pdf.

Maynard, T., Waters, J. & Clement, J. (2013). Moving outdoors: further explorations of 'child- initiated' learning in the outdoor environment. Education 3–13, 41 (3), 282–299.

Morgan, A. & Waite, S. (2017) Nestling into the world: The importance of place and mutuality in the early years. In: V. Huggins and D. Evans (eds.), *Early Childhood Education and Care for Sustainability*, TACTYC series. Abingdon: Routledge, pp. 51–66.

National Health Service (England) (2018) New mental health support in schools and colleges and faster access to NHS care. Available online at: https://www.england.nhs.uk/mental-health/cyp/trailblazers/.

Natural England (2013) Learning together: Schools and the natural environment sector. Available online at: publications.naturalengland.org.uk/file/4781669567430656.

Ofsted (2013) Religious Education: realising the potential. Available online at: https://assets.publishing.service.gov.uk/government/uploads/system/uploads/attachment_data/file/413157/Religious_education_-_realising_the_potential.pdf.

Ofsted (2018) An investigation into how to assess the quality of education through curriculum intent, implementation and impact: Phase 3 findings of curriculum research. Available online at: https://assets.publishing.service.gov.uk/government/uploads/system/uploads/attachment_data/file/766252/How_to_assess_intent_and_implementation_of_curriculum_191218.pdf.

OnePoll (2018) Survey for Decathlon. Available online at: www.dailymail.co.uk/sciencetech/article-5985661/Average-child-spends-just-7-hours-WEEK-outside-twice-playing-video-games.html.

Opie, M., Ansell, K. & Goto, E. (2017) Technology and its role outside the classroom. In: Waite, S. (ed.) *Children Learning Outside the Classroom: From birth to eleven. (2nd edition)*. London: SAGE, pp. 106–117.

Outdoor and Woodland Learning Scotland (2017) Tool Use guidance. Available online at: https://www.owlscotland.org/resources/resource-library/tool-use-guidance.

Paniagua, A. & Istance, D. (2018) Teachers as Designers of Learning Environments: The Importance of Innovative Pedagogies. Paris: Educational Research and Innovation, OECD Publishing. Available online at: https://doi.org/10.1787/9789264085374-en.

Porter, H. (2018) *Educating Outside: Curriculum-linked outdoor learning ideas for primary teachers*. London: Bloomsbury.

Public Health England (2014a) Improving access to green spaces. Health Equity Briefing 8. London: PHE.

Public Health England (2014b) The link between pupil health and wellbeing and attainment. A briefing for head teachers, governors and staff in education settings. London: PHE.

Religious Education Council of England and Wales (REC) (2013) A Curriculum Framework for Religious Education in England. Available online at: https://www.religiouseducationcouncil.org.uk/wp-content/uploads/2017/09/RE_Review_Summary.pdf.

Robb, M., Mew, V. & Richardson, A. (2015) *Learning with Nature*. Cambridge: Green Books.

Robertson, J. (2014) *Dirty Teaching: A Beginner's Guide to Learning Outdoors*. Carmarthen: Independent Thinking Press.

Rowe, S. & Humphries, S. (2012) *The Coombes Approach: Learning through an Experiential and Outdoor Curriculum*. London: Continuum.

Schofield, J. & Danks, F. (2009) *Go Wild!* London: Frances Lincoln Publishers Ltd.

Schofield, J. & Danks, F. (2012) *The Stick Book*. London: Frances Lincoln Publishers Ltd.

Training and Development Agency for Schools (TDA) (2009)

Including children with SEN and/or disabilities in primary physical education. Available online at: https://dera.ioe.ac.uk/13804/1/physicaleducationpe.pdf.

Tuke-Hastings, T., Shireen, N., Gupta, S. & Knight, J. (2011) *Cool Camping Cookbook*. Berlin: Haffmans and Tolkemitt.

Waite, S. (2010) Losing our way? The downward path for outdoor learning for children aged 2–11 years. *Journal of Adventure Education and Outdoor Learning*, 10 (2), 111–126.

Waite (2013) 'Knowing your place in the world': how place and culture support and obstruct educational aims. *Cambridge Journal of Education*, 43 (4), 413-434.

Waite, S., Davis, B. & Brown, K. (2006) *Five Stories of Outdoor Learning from Settings for 2–11 year olds in Devon*. Plymouth: University of Plymouth.

Waite, S., Passy, R., Gilchrist, M., Hunt, A. & Blackwell, I. (2016) Natural Connections Demonstration Project 2012–2016: Final report. Natural England Commissioned report NECR215. Available online at: http://publications.naturalengland.org.uk/publication/6636651036540928.

Waite, S., Passy, R. & Gilchrist, M. (2014) Getting it off PAT: researching the use of urban nature in schools. In: E. Backman, B. Humberstone & C. Loynes (2014) *Urban nature: inclusive learning through youth work and school work*. European Outdoor Education Network, Stockholm: Recito Forlag, pp. 35-49.

Waite, S., Rutter, O., Fowle, A. & Edwards-Jones, A. (2017) Diverse aims, challenges and opportunities for assessing outdoor learning: a critical examination of three cases from practice. *Education 3-13: International Journal of Primary, Elementary and Early Years Education*, 45 (1), 51–67.

Waite, S., Wickett, K. & Huggins, V. (2014) Risky outdoor play: Embracing uncertainty in pursuit of learning. In: T. Maynard and J. Waters (eds.) *Exploring Outdoor Play in the Early Years*. London: Open University Press, pp. 71–85.

Weiner, B. (1986). *An Attributional Theory of Motivation and Emotion*. New York: Springer-Verlag.

Wild Tribe Outdoor Learning programme (2019) Available online at: https://www.arena-schools.co.uk/wild-tribe.

Wood, C., Bragg, R. & Pretty, J. (2016) The benefits of green exercise for children. In: J. Barton, R. Bragg, C. Wood & J. Pretty (eds.) *Green Exercise: Linking Nature, Health and Well-being*. London: Routledge, pp. 46–52.

Woodland Trust Scotland (no date) Outdoor learning pack. Available online at: https://www.woodlandtrust.org.uk/media/43645/outdoor-learning-resource-pack.pdf.

Wright, N., Waite, S., Graham, L., Aronsson, J. & Waite, R. (2016) *Creating Happy and Healthy Schools through Outdoor Learning*. Plymouth: University of Plymouth. Hard copies available on request or online at: www.plymouth.ac.uk/research/peninsula-research-in-outdoor-learning/resources.

York Consulting (2015) Final evaluation of Learning Away: full report. Available online at: https://www.phf.org.uk/publications/learning-away-final-evaluation-full-report/. See also: https://learningaway.org.uk.

Minibeasts hunt sheet – Chasse aux petites bêtes

Add your own images below	Français	English	Tally
	un cloporte	woodlouse	
	une araignée	spider	
	un mille-pattes	millipede or centipede	
	une mouche	fly	
	un scarabée	beetle	
	un papillon	butterfly	
	une chenille	caterpillar	
	une fourmi	ant	
	un ver	worm	
	un escargot	snail	
	une limace	slug	
	une coccinelle	ladybird	
	une abeille	bee	